NEW DIRECTIONS FOR COMMUNITY COLLEGES

Arthur M. Cohen   Florence B. Brawer
EDITOR-IN-CHIEF   *ASSOCIATE EDITOR*

Pam Schuetz
PUBLICATION COORDINATOR

D0367000

Successful Approaches to Fundraising and Development

Mark David Milliron
Gerardo E. de los Santos
Boo Browning
League for Innovation in the Community College

EDITORS

Number 124, Winter 2003

JOSSEY-BASS
San Francisco

SUCCESSFUL APPROACHES TO FUNDRAISING AND DEVELOPMENT
Mark David Milliron, Gerardo E. de los Santos, Boo Browning (eds.)
New Directions for Community Colleges, no. 124

Arthur M. Cohen, Editor-in-Chief
Florence B. Brawer, Associate Editor

New Directions for Community Colleges is indexed in Current Index to Journals in Education (ERIC).

Microfilm copies of issues and articles are available in 16mm and 35mm, as well as microfiche in 105mm, through University Microfilms Inc., 300 North Zeeb Road, Ann Arbor, Michigan 48106-1346.

NEW DIRECTIONS FOR COMMUNITY COLLEGES (ISSN 0194-3081, electronic ISSN 1536-0733) is part of The Jossey-Bass Higher and Adult Education Series and is published quarterly by Wiley Subscription Services, Inc., A Wiley Company, at Jossey-Bass, 989 Market Street, San Francisco, California 94103-1741. Periodicals Postage Paid at San Francisco, California, and at additional mailing offices. POSTMASTER: Send address changes to New Directions for Community Colleges, Jossey-Bass, 989 Market Street, San Francisco, California 94103-1741.

SUBSCRIPTIONS cost $80.00 for individuals and $165.00 for institutions, agencies, and libraries. Prices subject to change.

EDITORIAL CORRESPONDENCE should be sent to the Editor-in-Chief, Arthur M. Cohen, at the Graduate School of Education and Information Studies, University of California, Box 951521, Los Angeles, California 90095-1521. All manuscripts receive anonymous reviews by external referees.

Cover photograph © Rene Sheret, After Image, Los Angeles, California, 1990.

CONTENTS

EDITORS' NOTES   1
Mark David Milliron, Gerardo E. de los Santos, Boo Browning

1. Strategies for Leveraging a Community College Foundation   5
Brenda Babitz
Community college foundations can achieve success by developing an expanded platform for philanthropic growth.

2. From the Foundations Up: Contexts for Change in   15
Community College Advancement
David Bass
The timing looks to be just right for community colleges to thrive under changes in the public funding of higher education.

3. It's Not the Race I Signed Up For, But It's the Race I'm In: 27
The Role of Community College Presidents
J. William Wenrich, Betheny L. Reid
With a shift in the fundraising landscape, college presidents and foundation CEOs are learning what a powerful team they can make.

4. The Role of Community College Trustees in Supporting the   33
Foundation
Norm Nielsen, Wayne Newton, Cheryle W. Mitvalsky
Four principles can help trustees support foundation efforts without neglecting other responsibilities to the college.

5. The Role of the President in Supporting the College's   41
Foundation
E. Ann McGee
Presidential leadership plays a pivotal role in a successful foundation.

6. Weaving the Foundation into the Culture of a Community   47
College
Charles J. Carlsen
Presidential leadership and involvement within the community promotes fundraising opportunities.

7. Generating New Sources of Revenue 53
Tony Zeiss
In the shift from being public supported to being privately supported, community colleges are learning to become educational enterprises.

8. Grants Development in Community Colleges 63
Neil Herbkersman, Karla Hibbert-Jones
A grants development office can raise significant amounts of funding when it is perceived as an integral component of the college.

9. Keeping in Touch: Alumni Development in Community 75
Colleges
Mark J. Pastorella
When a college understands how to cultivate, engage, and retain its alumni, it discovers the path to financial health.

10. Feels Like the Third Wave: The Rise of Fundraising in 81
the Community College
Mark David Milliron, Gerardo E. de los Santos, Boo Browning
Community colleges are new to the high-stakes fundraising game, but there are solid models from which they can learn important principles.

11. Sources and Information: Development and Fundraising 95
Within Community Colleges
Edward Francis Ryan
This chapter summarizes resources from the literature on development and fundraising.

INDEX 105

EDITORS' NOTES

Looking at the fundraising picture for higher education over the last ten years, one would have to argue that there have been major successes in garnering support from the private sector for educational institutions (Babitz, 2001; Reid, 2000). From billion-dollar capital campaigns to individuals donating millions for medical research and other educational activities, record support for higher education is at hand. However, in the midst of this community largesse, community colleges have not fared as well. Their traditional funding streams—local taxation, state funding, and federal programs—have begun to dry up (Roueche, Roueche, and Johnson, 2002), and they are increasingly turning to fundraising as a major method to support their vital missions to provide open-access and high-quality postsecondary education (Milliron and de los Santos, in press). Many community colleges are relatively new to fundraising and are just beginning to develop tools, techniques, and strategies that make sense for them. This volume outlines key contextual issues in institutional advancement, provides success strategies from institutions that have successfully addressed fundraising over the last ten years, and outlines major issues for those interested in community college fundraising.

We engage a broad range of authors to take on this task, and what follows is a big-picture look at college fundraising and development issues. The reader will likely notice that many of these chapters reflect emerging best practices and strategies more than detailed research on the topic. Given the lack of longstanding programs and active research protocols in community college fundraising, this tack seemed most appropriate.

In Chapter One, Brenda Babitz uses Monroe Community College in Rochester, New York, as a prime example to explore the role of a foundation in support of a community college. An important aspect of this chapter is its examination of how a successful community college advancement program practices an institutionwide responsibility for fundraising. With a specific focus on strategies that work in the community college sector—scholarships, business partnerships, and broader institutional support—Babitz describes how a community college can truly build on its foundation.

In Chapter Two, David Bass outlines key differences between the university and community college sectors that must be considered by community college fundraisers as they take steps forward to prepare their initiatives. With years of experience in this arena, the Council for the Advancement and Support of Education (CASE) is unequaled in its programming for college foundations. However, its leadership is also clear that there are distinguishing community college foundation dynamics that make applying traditional university models difficult, if not impossible.

William Wenrich and Betheny Reid, in Chapter Three, describe how many senior community college presidents express the same sentiment: fundraising was not a major part of the job when they became presidents, but now it is beginning to dominate their time. The authors examine the changing role of the community college CEO, particularly focusing on how fundraising is becoming a major expectation for community college leaders. Strategies to perform this role well are shared, as well as ideas for keeping the fundraising activities from interfering with the day-to-day operations of the college.

Chapter Four analyzes the relationship between the trustees of the college and the trustees of the foundation. Norm Nielsen, Wayne Newton, and Cheryle Mitvalsky examine the overlapping yet often distinct role that institutional trustees can play in supporting their college's foundation and foundation board members. Moreover, there is the responsibility of foundation trustees to support the core mission of the institution and to coordinate efforts with institutional trustees.

Drawing on their experiences as college presidents, the authors of Chapters Five and Six offer insight into how leadership and involvement from the president creates successful foundations and development opportunities. They discuss how bringing foundation activities into the mainstream culture of an institution is imperative; building support, involving staff and faculty, and communicating ongoing activities are topics specifically addressed. In Chapter Five, Ann McGee describes successful strategies used as a foundation director and college president and discusses the pivotal role of the president in promoting the foundation. In Chapter Six, Charles Carlsen discusses the importance of presidential leadership and involvement within the community and explores the role of the president as enabler and leader in promoting fundraising opportunities.

In Chapter Seven, Tony Zeiss focuses on successful community college practices in fundraising through four types of opportunities: educational enterprises, contracted services, business partnerships, and entrepreneurial activities. Examples of successful programs at colleges are highlighted, and Central Piedmont Community College (North Carolina) is discussed as a model of an enterprising college in terms of taking advantage of these opportunities.

Based on years of experience in supporting community college fundraising, and grant writing in particular, in Chapter Eight, Neil Herbkersman and Karla Hibbert-Jones represent the Council for Resource Development (an affiliate council of the American Association of Community Colleges) and explore strategies for obtaining grant funding to support community college programming and activities. A special focus is given to the dynamics between grants management and foundation management, and how these twin fundraising strategies can work together to advance a community college agenda.

Mark Pastorella, in Chapter Nine, describes distinctive strategies for defining and relating to alumni in community colleges, along with basic principles for ongoing community relations based on broad, comprehensive programming and relationship building. Defining community college alumni and building ongoing relationships with former community college students are difficult propositions. Community college programs are shorter than those at universities, and students often transfer or move on to work before certificates or degrees are obtained. Given these dynamics, traditional university models of alumni development are hard to apply in the community college context.

We argue in Chapter Ten that comprehensive and institutionwide fundraising and advancement efforts are an integral part of a fundamental shift and transition point for community colleges (Milliron and Neil, 2003). We compare Toffler's (1989) work on transformation and the "third wave" framework to our own transitions surrounding fundraising and advancement in community colleges. While we may not be making as huge a leap as Toffler suggests that broader society has made in the move from the agrarian age (first wave) to the industrial age (second wave) to the information age (third wave), community and technical colleges have experienced their own waves of change. The authors in this chapter outline key community college waves, including comprehensive integration of academic and vocational programming (our first wave), entrepreneurial expansion and workforce development (our second wave), and now institutional advancement and fundraising (our third wave). Finally, we argue that the third wave is a welcome transition for community colleges, enhancing their role as fully engaged partners in their communities.

In Chapter Eleven, the concluding chapter, Edward Ryan summarizes resources from the literature on fundraising and development activities, the role of various constituencies in the fundraising and development process, and the best practices that have emerged.

Mark David Milliron
Gerardo E. de los Santos
Boo Browning
Editors

References

Babitz, B. "Building on Your Foundation." *Leadership Abstracts*, 2001, *14*(4). [http://www.league.org/publication/abstracts/leadership/labs0801.html]. Accessed Oct. 8, 2003.

Milliron, M., and de los Santos, G. "Making the Most of Community Colleges on the Road Ahead." *Community College Journal of Research and Practice*, *28*(2), forthcoming.

Milliron, M., and Neil, W. *What Do CEOs Want to Know About Key Trends in the Community College?* Phoenix, Ariz.: League for Innovation in the Community College, 2003.

Reid, B. "Rising Star: A Community College Foundation at Work." *Leadership Abstracts,* 2000, *13*(6). [http://www.league.org/publication/abstracts/leadership/labs1200.htm]. Accessed Oct. 8, 2003.

Roueche, J., Roueche, S., and Johnson, R. "At Our Best: Facing the Challenges." *Community College Journal,* 2002, *72*(5), 10–14.

Toffler, A. *The Third Wave.* New York: Random House, 1989.

MARK DAVID MILLIRON *is president and CEO of the League for Innovation in the Community College.*

GERARDO E. DE LOS SANTOS *is vice president and COO of the League for Innovation in the Community College.*

BOO BROWNING *is associate editor at the League for Innovation in the Community College.*

1

*While community college foundations may be the new
kids on the fundraising block, they are well positioned to
build private-sector support. This chapter discusses ways
foundations can achieve success by developing a platform
for expanded philanthropic growth.*

Strategies for Leveraging a Community College Foundation

Brenda Babitz

Over the past two centuries, the United States has emerged as a pioneer, prototype, and worldwide champion for modern philanthropy. Almost every aspect of American life—from education to health, the arts, and social programs—has been supported and enriched by private-sector involvement. Yet only within the past generation have our nation's more than 1,200 community colleges begun to share in this harvest of contributions and support.

The recognition of community colleges as worthy recipients of support from corporations, foundations, individuals, and the community itself is a new phenomenon that could not have come at a more opportune time. Across America, the baby-boom echo is reaching college age, a new wave of immigrants and first-generation students is looking to higher education as the springboard to a better life, and millions of workers face the need to upgrade skill levels or be left behind among the downsized.

But this confluence of demographic and economic trends that is placing unprecedented demands on our two-year colleges comes at a time of economic uncertainty, a volatile stock market, and a decline at every level of government's ability to fund American higher education. The bottom line, as the Association of Governing Boards reminds us, is that we have the challenge of doing more for many more with much less (Wellman, 2002).

This is a time when private-sector involvement can help bridge the gap and, understandably, corporations, foundations, and individuals are being pressed to give more generously than ever before. In fact, as the number of nonprofit organizations continues to proliferate, the competition to attract volunteer leadership, sponsorships, and gifts has intensified. An article in the *Chronicle of Higher Education* states, "Over the last decade, almost all of the country's 1,100 community colleges have begun fundraising. Some with great success. They are beginning to compete with larger institutions for foundation money. The money supplements operating budgets, and many colleges are building endowments that enable them to offer scholarships and keep student costs low" (van der Werf, 1999, p. A42–A43).

The good news is, despite an uncertain economy and volatile financial markets, the transfer of wealth from one generation to the next in the United States over the next twenty years is projected to exceed $41 trillion (Havens and Schervish, 2003). Moreover, this wealth transfer comes just as the private sector is beginning to appreciate the case for America's community colleges: our ability to innovate and adapt; our shared commitment to educational access; our growing impact on community well-being; and our particular capacity to meet the workforce training needs of businesses large and small.

In short, if the levels of access and instructional quality needed to maintain America's skilled workforce—and by extension our nation's competitive edge—are to be ensured, then private-sector investment in public higher education must continue to increase. Community colleges have an obligation to succeed. The stakes are high and the message is clear. There can be no doubt that the future belongs to community colleges that can adapt new strategies and new solutions to alleviate funding pressures.

The task then is for community college foundations to engage the private sector, underscoring that their college is the vital link between today's students and tomorrow's workforce. Indeed, it is only by involving corporations, foundations, and individuals in the compelling work of community-based learning that community college foundations can put a fair share of this new wealth to work.

The Quest for Private Support

Even today, fundraising at the community college level remains a relatively new and untested phenomenon. The *Community College Journal* reports that colleges across the nation are implementing strategies, created by necessity, with enormously promising results (Roueche, Roueche, and Johnson, 2002). Their fundraising has become an established college activity, often referred to as *friendraising* when initiatives and partnerships pay off.

The prerequisite task for the community college foundation is to develop a case for support, then get that case on the giving agenda of corporations and others that have traditionally viewed funding for community-based education as the province of state and local governments alone. At the same time, community colleges must create an organizationwide atmosphere for giving, an environment that both fosters and celebrates the philanthropic impulse. The more powerfully community college foundations speak to the importance of fundraising and philanthropy, the greater the potential to raise interest, emotions, and expectations in the minds of our donors and prospects.

While the vast majority of community colleges have operating foundations, the Council for Aid to Education's *2002 Voluntary Support of Education* (Kaplan, 2003) reports that most of these foundations are small in terms of revenue raised and overall impact. Of the ninety-two community colleges responding, however, thirty-three schools reported total gifts over $1 million. Those reporting current (not deferred) gifts of $1 million or more for each of the past two years include community colleges such as Santa Barbara (California), Delta (Michigan), Broward (Florida), SUNY Monroe, Morrisville, and Suffolk (New York), Montgomery (Maryland), Norwalk (Connecticut), and Cabrillo (California). These institutions have organized their foundations to support a total advancement program, adapting practices once exclusive to four-year schools and universities. Most have developed a fundraising mix that includes annual funds and capital campaigns, special events and planned giving, donor stewardship activities, and alumni outreach.

Michael J. Worth notes that "successful fundraising efforts capitalize on strengths and untapped potential of institutions in direct response to institutional needs and capabilities" (as cited in Keener, 1997, p. 188). To support the diverse range of fundraising initiatives, foundation leaders must set standards for integrity, develop clear expectations for roles and responsibilities, and achieve operational effectiveness. But what are the essential keys to success?

The Fundraising Process

First, successful foundation advancement officers must develop a clear understanding of the fundraising process. They must build a board consisting of the right people. They must involve corporate leaders in their mission, knowing that those who participate are most likely to contribute financially. Appreciating that people give to people, they should involve their foundation board in campus activities that complement each member's business acumen or specific interest.

Knowing, too, that most donors like to give to those who help themselves, it is important to develop support from within the institutional family, including faculty, staff, trustees, and directors, for the foundation's strategic plan. The institutional family should be involved in the fundraising plan and asked to contribute before other constituencies.

Moreover, the college family has a story to tell to others. People give to organizations that are accountable. Successful community college foundations work with their institutions to fully understand where the college is going and what private funds are needed to get there. They should integrate their alumni into their overall fundraising structure, recognizing the foundation's potential as a vehicle for keeping alumni and friends involved and inspiring current students with stories of alumni successes.

Developing an organizational creed of ethical practices with policies and procedures is critical in today's challenging marketplace. Donor contributions must be used to further the institution's mission and satisfy the specific intent of donors. By managing resources wisely, ethics and accountability will become an integral part of the foundation's culture. Successful community college foundations recognize the importance of stewardship, knowing full well that donor loyalty and ongoing commitment requires much more than fundraising strategies alone.

An Institutionwide Responsibility

A successful community college advancement program has defined roles for each segment of the college family, including faculty, staff, and even students. But the major responsibilities are in the hands of the trustees, the president, the chief advancement officer, and the foundation board.

The Trustees. The college's trustees are critical to the advancement process. As the governing body, trustees have traditionally been held responsible for fiscal planning and policies at the highest level. Yet today's trustees, faced with a need for resources beyond those funded by public-sector budgets each year, should explore new sources of revenue generation, first by authorizing the creation of an institutionally related foundation, then by approving the foundation's long-range plans, supporting its activities, and acting as public advocates for the foundation.

The College President. Serving as the central link between trustees and the foundation, the college president must work to assure that relationships between these policy-making groups are dynamic and synergistic, reflecting mutual respect and a clear understanding of shared and distinctive responsibilities. All such relationships should be clarified in writing, with fundraising policies adopted by mutual consent and long-range plans implemented only with governing board approval.

As the guiding hand and voice for the institution, college presidents are also their campuses' most vital and visible fundraising presence. They must develop an institutional vision that is forward looking and sustainable, ensure that their chief advancement officer is well qualified, maintain strong ties with the foundation board, understand the development process, cultivate and solicit major gift prospects, and attend foundation-sponsored activities.

The Chief Advancement Officer (CAO). It is the CAO, often the foundation executive, who must make this all work. As a member of the college's senior management team, the CAO must actively participate in institutional strategic planning. With support from the college in the form of personnel and resources, the chief advancement officer works with the foundation board to develop and implement fundraising policies, programs, and strategies that benefit the institution.

The CAO must take the lead in identifying, recruiting, training, and effectively using each member of the foundation's volunteer board; oversee both annual and long-range planning; motivate staff and volunteers; evaluate programs and human resources; and follow up on a myriad of details to help the foundation succeed. Advancement staff must be seen as consummate professionals and should be integrated fully within the academic setting.

The Foundation Board. Community college foundations are established as not-for-profit corporations that solicit, receive, and disburse private funds. They derive their authority and legitimacy from the institutions with which they are affiliated. A successful development program requires the foundation to balance its autonomy with an appropriate degree of accountability to the governing board.

In earlier years, community college foundation boards were socially oriented, with few members experienced in the dynamics of fundraising. David Pierce, former president and chief executive officer of the American Association of Community Colleges, notes that the earliest foundations were formed to own real estate or to run enterprises that were neither state mandated nor funded. By the mid-1980s, only a handful reported raising $1 million or more. Board giving itself was insubstantial. Those colleges that established annual giving programs provided a means for board members to cultivate prospects and solicit meaningful-sized contributions. In those years, however, state and local funding was more than adequate, and contributions from the private sector, while welcomed, were rarely needed (as cited in Keener, 1997).

By contrast, today's highly competitive philanthropic environment demands board members who are strongly committed to the institution, which manifests in their own leadership-level generosity. New directors need to become knowledgeable about the college and its mission in order to advise and support the college president and chief advancement officer. Acting as ambassadors for the college, board members should be willing to identify, cultivate, and solicit potential donors. They must be willing to lead by example and personally invest in the college and its programs—all while carrying out the board's fiduciary responsibility.

How and where do you find such individuals? And once you identify them, how do you recruit them, retain their interest, and make best use of their individual strengths and abilities? Therein lies an ambitious challenge for both the president and the chief advancement officer.

Understandably, the influence and effectiveness of a foundation board begin with the reputation, capabilities, and commitment of its members. While every rule has exceptions, experience teaches that effective board members most often share one or more of the following characteristics: personal wealth, a tradition of public service, a high level of corporate or professional achievement, or a leadership role in other community development activities. A relationship with the institution, either personal or corporate, is always desirable.

To be productive, the foundation must have a viable plan and structure for board activities. Such a framework encourages the development of strong leadership and shared goals. It provides the opportunity for the CAO to engage the talents and interests of each member to the foundation's best advantage. Accordingly, to build a stronger board, the CAO must give high priority to board recruitment, orientation, and retention activities. This includes the ability to identify skills as well as attributes, determine meaningful committee assignments, and build relationships that will ultimately lead to increased support.

Specific Strategies to Build Support

College foundations should incorporate a number of strategies and activities to ensure effective fundraising. The strategies discussed below derive from the experiences of the Monroe Community College (MCC) Foundation in Rochester, New York.

Annual Fund. The annual fund can be counted on to help support immediate as well as long-term needs. Direct mail, telemarketing, and personal solicitations are all effective ways to reach out to friends of the college, many of whom can be counted on for gifts of $500, $1,000, or more each year. These friends may include parents, present staff and faculty, retirees, vendors, graduate employees, alumni, small and large businesses, and college leaders such as trustees and foundation directors.

Special Events. While time consuming in their preparation, special events advance positive perceptions of the college and are useful for friendraising as well as fundraising. Events that involve or honor prominent figures from the worlds of business, politics, and entertainment tend to draw the most interest within a community. Communitywide programs that include award ceremonies work well to validate the college's educational purposes while helping recognize those alumni and special individuals who have made the college a better place.

The MCC Foundation developed an executive spelling bee that brought corporate leaders to the college stage and, ultimately, to the funding table. This type of event provides an opportunity to expose new people to the college and grow a list of donors and volunteers. Golf tournaments can be used to cultivate new friends for the college while raising needed scholarship funds. Securing sponsorships—especially those with local ties—can virtually guarantee a tournament's success on both the social and fundraising levels. Dinner auctions featuring wine tasting and gourmet food are used by community colleges to raise money for scholarships. These types of events may feature silent and live auction segments that draw on the skills of the institutional family. Faculty and staff may be eager to donate their services or expertise as an auction item—such as private French lessons or fly-fishing with the president. Within an atmosphere of camaraderie, the college's faculty and leadership will influence other guests to support the college's students. Live auctions have built-in entertainment value as the bids increase over select items.

Focused Initiatives. Foundation support of specific academic and campus-life projects, establishing chairs in specific disciplines, or developing a groundbreaking program that draws in expertise from beyond the college campus may provide that added incentive for donors and volunteers to become involved. MCC's Holocaust Genocide Studies Project, for example, draws interest from throughout the region as it brings internationally renowned speakers to its programs and donors to the MCC Foundation. An annual grants competition for faculty and staff ensures that innovation remains part of the MCC experience and new ideas receive the funding they need to become reality.

Capital Campaign. Capital campaign initiatives must strive for a higher goal than other ongoing fundraising activities yet complement them as well. Campaigns provide an additional option for people to donate to the college foundation and become involved in securing the college's future. Campaign success relies on careful study, planning, and identification of major potential donors. By communicating specific goals and how those goals will benefit students and the community in which they live, campaigns can be used to lay the groundwork for involvement of new volunteers and donors and set the stage for higher annual giving levels.

Planned Gifts. Planned giving, or charitable gift planning, refers to the process of making a charitable gift of estate assets that requires consideration and planning in light of the donor's overall estate plan. Consider establishing a planned giving society, named in honor of a founding trustee or other highly recognizable person within the college's history. Granting membership within the society should be designed to honor and recognize individuals who have made a charitable planned gift or who have made known their intentions to include a college foundation within a will or estate plan. Listing of society members and invitation-only social events can be used to make these special donors feel appreciated. Educating constituencies through a specialized newsletter promoting the benefits of planned giving to a potential donor and his or her family may help to encourage people to consider this giving option.

Alumni Giving. New paradigms are being created by community colleges that encourage alumni involvement. Welcome alumni representation on the foundation board. Honor those alumni who have achieved personal and professional excellence by nominating them to an alumni hall of fame. Recognize new alumni during commencement exercises and ask them to immediately give back through service to the college and to participate in a welcoming program for the next class of new students. Develop an alumni website to connect alumni with the college community. Alumni are grateful for the opportunities afforded by their community colleges, and a good advancement program learns to capitalize on their success. Contrary to what people may believe, alumni who have received advanced degrees do want to give credit to their community college, often indicating that "it's the community college that inspired them to achieve and gave them their first glimpse of what education could do for their lives" (Machanic, 2002, p. 5).

Donor Stewardship. Donor stewardship initiatives work to build and reinforce loyalty through recognition activities; the awarding of philanthropic medals; prominently displayed donor recognition boards; and named endowments, teaching chairs, and new facilities. Effective stewardship—making donors and friends aware of the impact and value of private gifts—is a vital component of private giving, energizing and informing both the community at large and those who make gifts (Hedgepeth, 2003). As a donor base grows, the foundation may choose to sponsor more targeted, invitation-only leadership events.

Communications. An ongoing communications program helps to keep donors and volunteers informed and connected with the foundation and the community college. It should incorporate the college's overall growth strategies and be tailored to individual constituencies. Annual fund letters and brochures, campaign materials, presentations, newsletters, videos, and annual reports should all tell the college story. Programs should promote the activities of major donors and strengthen the foundation's visual identity within its community. A video profiling successful alumni can help to educate donors and the community that their gifts can really pay the dividend of a changed life.

Marketing and Resource Development. No matter how sophisticated the fundraising strategy or investment policy, the effectiveness of the community college foundation is contingent on the institutional image. According to Keener, Ryan, and Smith (1991), the following are important elements in the development of a positive institutional image:

- Involvement of the college trustees, president, faculty, and staff in the community
- Experiences of local employers with students
- Services that are responsive to the needs of students and the community
- An attractive campus with well-groomed grounds and well-maintained buildings
- Most important, the quality of education received from the college

The significance of marketing and institutional image is further reinforced by a six-year study of community college fundraising, sponsored by the Council for Advancement and Support of Education. The study found that colleges that are the most successful in fundraising have two characteristics in common: a strong marketing program and widespread community support (Keener, Ryan, and Smith, 1991).

Management. An accountable framework for success is important. College leadership must recruit and invest in highly capable foundation staff. A comprehensive manual of policies and procedures must be developed to assist in decision making and work flow. Staff should focus toward energizing the board by activating new committee structures, providing extensive volunteer training, encouraging leadership generosity, and closely monitoring results. Central to the entire management process is a well-managed information system with accurate record keeping and timely gift acknowledgments.

In Summary

Now more than ever, foundations have the opportunity to develop new solutions to alleviate funding pressure by making it clear that the community colleges they support are meeting public needs and providing the link between today's student and tomorrow's workforce. Activities that focus on what the community and its neighborhoods would be like if the college never existed—in terms of economic vitality, quality of life, and even the people themselves—can help stimulate new sources of support.

Attract to the foundation members who have the desire, the enthusiasm, and the financial ability to benefit your college. Make certain to support experienced advancement officers. Help raise the giving sights among members of the institutional family by supporting the foundation and its mission. Embrace the college's mission and convey it to professional colleagues and community peers in order to help articulate the need for private-sector support. This will help to validate fundraising initiatives and encourage people to consider the foundation as a solid investment.

Today's 67- to 74-year-olds account for more than one-third of the nation's wealth. And their numbers—and assets—are growing. Many of these wealthy older Americans care deeply about their communities. Many have lived all their lives in the same town. Many are looking for a way to touch the face of tomorrow. Community college foundations hold a key to their immortality. Tell donors how to endow a teaching chair. Talk to them about scholarships and programs and the people who need them. Excite their charitable interests. Invite them to campus activities that showcase the best of the institution. Introduce them to students. Make them feel a part of the college family.

Today's community college foundations can play an increasingly pivotal role in funding the college's current needs and long-term aspirations, by working to validate the case for their institutions, recruiting volunteer leadership, building new donor constituencies, following sound board practices, and developing fresh revenue streams. Success has its building blocks: notably, a motivated president, a foundation board that is strongly committed, a comprehensive fundraising plan that effectively integrates the foundation's mission with that of the college, and an advancement program that both appreciates and capitalizes on the character of its community.

Colleges must build trust, respect, and confidence with the private sector. The foundation can be critical to this process. Together we must convince our communities that public higher education offers direct and indirect returns on investment that are as dramatic as they are compelling. There is no question that the fiscal challenges community colleges face are enormous, but even greater are the risks of inaction. Community college foundations must rise to the occasion and make positive change the new order of business.

References

Havens, J., and Schervish, P. "Why the $41 Trillion Wealth Transfer Estimate Is Still Valid: A Review of Challenges and Questions." *The Journal of Gift Planning*, 2003, 7(1), 11–15, 47–50.

Hedgepeth, R. "Proposed Transition Plan for Monroe Community College (MCCF '08)." Paper presented to the MCCF Board of Directors, Rochester, N.Y., Jan. 22, 2003.

Kaplan, A. E. *2002 Voluntary Support of Education*. New York: Council for Aid to Education, 2003.

Keener, B. J. "The Community College Foundation." In J. F. Phelan and Associates, *College and University Foundations: Serving America's Public Higher Education*. Washington, D.C.: Association of Governing Boards of Universities and Colleges, 1997.

Keener, B. J., Ryan, G. J., and Smith, N. J. "Paying Attention Pays Off." *Community, Technical and Junior College Journal*, 1991, 62, 34–37.

Machanic, K. "Alumni: A Valuable Resource." *Community College Times*, Nov. 12, 2002, p. 5.

Roueche, J. E., Roueche, S. D., and Johnson, R. A. "At Our Best: Facing the Challenge." *Community College Journal*, Apr.-May 2002, 72(5), 10–14.

van der Werf, M. "For Community Colleges, Fundraising Has Become Serious and Successful." *Chronicle of Higher Education*, Apr. 9, 1999, pp. A42-A43.

Wellman, J. "Weathering the Double Whammy." In Working Paper for the AGB National Conference on Trusteeship. Washington, D.C.: Association of Governing Boards of Universities and Colleges, 2002.

BRENDA BABITZ *is chief advancement officer at Monroe Community College in Rochester, New York, and president of the Monroe Community College Foundation. She has led the organization for twelve years, during which time the Foundation has raised $25 million.*

2

Unlike past fiscal crises and retrenchment, current changes in the funding of public higher education could precipitate fundamental changes in colleges and universities. Community colleges might be well positioned to thrive in such turbulent times.

From the Foundations Up: Contexts for Change in Community College Advancement

David Bass

The proposed title for this chapter was "A Tale of Two Foundations: Comparing Community College and University Advancement." Any such comparison would, however, be hopelessly reductive. College and university foundations are essentially idiosyncratic, reflecting the peculiarities of individual institutional cultures, state and system contexts, and financial and political circumstances. This diversity is perhaps even greater among community colleges that tend to be more closely governed by regional and community influences. The Dickensian dichotomy is, however, worth considering. The current winter of despair could prove a spring of hope for institutions capable not just of adapting but of finding opportunity in the current climate of change. As an important interface between public institutions and private constituents, foundations can play a vital role in facilitating institutional evolution.

The Best of Times and the Worst of Times

The fiscal year 2003 was, for most institutions of higher education, a season of despair. State appropriations plunged to new lows, endowment values dropped nearly 10 percent in 2001 and 2002, and voluntary support for higher education declined for the first time in fourteen years (Kaplan, 2003; National Association of College and University Business Officers, 2003). The largest endowments have generally performed the best. Endowments over $1 billion declined an average of 3.8 percent, while endowments of $25 million and less lost 6.6 percent on average. Reductions in state appropriations have disproportionately affected community colleges whose budgets rely more heavily on state funds than those of four-year institutions (Hebel, 2003a).

Many commentators are suggesting that the current recession, unlike previous fiscal crises, will compel public colleges and universities to change in potentially revolutionary ways and adapt to different assumptions about the meaning and means of public higher education. As the traditional class structure of higher education shifts, elite institutions will, for better or worse, increasingly yield to market interests; and community colleges, like so many Dickensian heroes endowed only with goodwill and wit, will encounter new challenges and great opportunities, if they are plucky enough to seize them.

Privatization

Mark Yudof, chancellor of the University of Texas System, has become the most distinguished prophet of the privatization of public higher education. He argues that current educational budget crises are one more manifestation of the long-term trends leading to the creation of what he calls the hybrid university. These institutions are less reliant on state appropriations and increasingly draw on philanthropic support, tuition, and other revenue sources. Despite increased financial independence, they are still subject to public regulation and oversight and charged with important public responsibilities.

Yudof (2002) states: "In order to adapt successfully to the current environment, public research universities will have to evolve. . . . charging higher tuition—though still much less than what their private peers charge—and looking to private sources for funds and partnerships. They must do so while retaining their essential public character" (p. 19).

The changes reshaping state universities create opportunities for other institutions as well. "The new, market-oriented model for higher education funding may provide all institutions with a better opportunity to explain their strength to the public and to compete on their own merits. Marketplaces are nothing if not pluralistic" (Yudof, 2003, p. 12). Although the hybrid university has much in common with for-profit business models, Yudof also sees it as creating "new avenues for philanthropy" that will play an increasingly important role in supporting public higher education.

Yudof is not alone in seeing the current hard times as a catalyst for structural change and possible opportunity. Clara Lovett (2002) and David Breneman (2002) have both compared the current financial crisis to the recessions of the 1970s, 1980s, and early 1990s. Both, however, see a fundamental difference in the twenty-first-century crisis. They suggest that outmoded tax structures, increased competition for state funds, and growing numbers of lower-income students have created a situation in which public colleges and universities will have to undergo radical structural changes along with changes in state taxation.

Gordon Davies (2003) similarly argues that state revenue shortfalls, which he estimates could surpass $85 billion in the 2003–04 fiscal year, will persist throughout the decade and entail fundamental changes in higher education: "The situation is clearly not encouraging, but it does offer opportunities. Significant reform in any enterprise, including higher education, rarely occurs in good economic times. . . . Most substantive change and improvement has come when money is scarce" (p. B20).

A report by the National Association of State Budget Officers confirms that this recession is unlike those of the early 1980s and 1990s. Last year, thirty-seven states made midyear budget cuts totaling $14.5 billion—the deepest in the twenty-seven-year history of the survey. Half of the states reduced spending on higher education, making cuts averaging 5 percent (Potter, 2003). Richard Novak, director of public-sector programs for the Association of Governing Boards of Universities and Colleges, suggests that colleges must begin "radically altering the way we do things. . . . The last recession wasn't deep enough, or didn't last long enough to take restructuring to the level needed. . . . We may come out of the other end of the tube with institutions looking very different" (as cited in Potter, 2003, p. A22).

Public Purpose

In the privatization of higher education, Robert Zemsky (2003), chairman of the Learning Alliance, sees an abandonment of state colleges and universities as "places of public purpose." Zemsky looks to California community colleges for a hypothetical alternative to self-serving privatization. Zemsky concludes that if the California colleges had been charged with creating counseling centers for newly arrived immigrants in exchange for less drastic budget cuts than the proposed reduction of 5.6 percent, the state would have sent the message that community colleges remain places of public purpose and service as well as self-supporting enterprises serving student consumers. Zemsky's decision to shift the focus of his article from four-year institutions and turn to community colleges for an example is telling. Fiscal and market conditions driving privatization will make it increasingly hard for state institutions of all types to focus on missions dictated by public interest, but community colleges might be particularly well suited to adapt.

Community colleges have always sought to ensure access to higher education by maintaining open admission policies and charging low tuition. They also serve their communities and promote economic growth and prosperity by providing remedial education, continuing education, and workforce training tailored to the needs of local industries. In addition to these core missions, community colleges have increasingly forged partnerships with local businesses, nonprofits, and government agencies that foster community ties and contribute to economic development and college revenue.

In these and other ways, community colleges are fundamentally "places of public purpose." At the same time, their focus on service to students, community organizations, and local business has led them to embody practices associated with privatization, including adopting a culture of service to the student as a client, adapting programs in response to market changes, and customizing niche marketing curricula for local industry and business. Although Yudof's conception of privatization envisions changes to research and regional universities, community colleges clearly face similar challenges and, arguably, are much better equipped to adapt in ways that will allow them to compete with private for-profit institutions and remain true to their core values of accessibility and service.

In February and March of 2003, the *Chronicle of Higher Education* conducted 1,000 interviews, finding strong support for public higher education (Selingo, 2003). Ninety-one percent of respondents agreed or strongly agreed that colleges and universities are one of the country's most valuable resources. While the public broadly agrees that colleges and universities are valuable, only half of Americans see a four-year degree as essential to success in society. Eighty-two percent agreed or strongly agreed that "it is very difficult for a middle-class family to afford a college education," and 67 percent think that state and federal governments should invest more money in higher education. Forty-two percent of respondents said community colleges in their states are of high or very high quality and expressed essentially the same level of confidence in them as in public four-year institutions—a level of confidence substantially higher than that earned by public elementary and high schools. Given a list of twenty-one roles that colleges could perform, 92 percent of respondents ranked preparing undergraduate students for a career important or very important. Providing education to adults so they qualify for better jobs was ranked second, with 90 percent of the respondents ranking it important or very important (Selingo, 2003). Patrick Callan, president of the National Center for Public Policy and Higher Education, suggests the data indicates that "community colleges are moving into the mainstream of what Americans think of when they think higher education. . . . They are no longer the third cousins" (as cited in Selingo, 2003, p. A10).

Americans' belief that education is necessary for both personal advancement and the growth of the economy, their concern about the cost of higher education, and ongoing demographic shifts suggest that the market for community colleges is only going to increase. Although it may be the worst of times for funding and finances, it may be the best of times from a market perspective. In recent years, states have set aside resources for research-related projects that would build public universities' expertise in commercially lucrative fields even as they have cut operating funds and financial aid (Hebel, 2003b). While the emphasis on the economic value of research does not bode well for community college funding, the results of the "Chronicle Survey of Public Opinion on Higher Education" (2003) as well as rising enrollment rates, suggest a wealth of opportunities for growth. As Oregon University System Chancellor Richard Jarvis suggests, "Adding research programs isn't the only way that colleges can help states economically. Supporting programs that help adults finish a degree or that retrain them for better jobs . . . often can meet work-force needs faster" (as cited in Hebel, 2003b). How can community colleges overcome fiscal challenges and best take advantage of current opportunities? The answers are probably as numerous as community colleges themselves. Lessons learned from the private sector and adapted by four-year institutions and the untapped potential of affiliated foundations will probably play a central role in whatever strategies local circumstances suggest.

State University Models and Community Contexts

Almost twenty years ago, Michael Worth described the emerging symbiotic relationship between institutional advancement, increased voluntary support, and public-private partnerships. "State governments will increasingly encourage their colleges' and universities' efforts to build partnerships with the private sector. . . . Public universities, as well as community colleges, have a distinct opportunity here" (1985, p. 11). In *New Strategies for Educational Fund Raising,* Worth (2002) again surveys the landscape of educational advancement, looking at demographics, technology, globalization, and the dominance of market thinking. Despite the enormous changes that have taken place in the past two decades, he concludes with the observation that "the more things change, the more at least some things stay the same" (p. xxix). Other scholars and commentators have made similar claims.

In 1991, John Blong and Barb Bennett argued that "state appropriations will never again provide sufficient funds to encourage and support innovation and excellence in higher education. . . . resource development, planning, and management functions will be of paramount importance in the successful community college of the 1990s" (p. 32). Seven years later, Glass and Jackson (1998) echoed this: "Reduced financial support and increased demands have created an environment in which community colleges have had to eliminate programs, cut back service, or seek ways to enhance revenue. . . . To be successful, the resource development function should be aligned with the college's vision and mission; integrated into the mainstream of college planning and management" (pp. 715, 734).

In 2002, Barbara Keener, Sharon Carrier, and Sherry Meaders again observed that "in an era of declining core state and local tax support, public community colleges have begun to rely more on external revenue sources for basic operations" (p. 8). They conclude that "resource development as an integrated function with today's community college will be critical for the future vitality of community colleges" (p. 22).

As this brief history suggests, commentators, scholars, and practitioners have long agreed that community colleges need to cultivate increased private support. Strong presidential leadership, institutional commitment, and commitment of financial resources have been identified as fundamental to successful development efforts along with sustained marketing and the cultivation of strategic alliances with local business and industry.

A glance at the organizational chart of even a modest four-year institution's advancement office and that of a large community college suggests, however, that community colleges cannot simply reproduce the advancement and marketing strategies typical of four-year institutions. Four-year institutions and their foundations might have professional staff devoted to alumni affairs, the annual fund, planned giving, corporate and foundation relations, and communications. They might have finance as well as major-gift officers, unit development officers, and technical and administrative support. At a community college, one or two staff members might be responsible for all advancement functions. In their insightful discussion of resource development and institutional planning, Glass and Jackson (1998) argue that "two-year public institutions have been encouraged to adopt models developed by senior institutions: setting up an advancement function, emphasizing solicitations from corporations rather than alumni donors, developing an annual giving program, and emulating more aggressive fundraising practices. . . . Few community colleges, however, use the formal highly structured institutional advancement and fundraising models found in university settings." They go on to consider institutional advancement as a process focused on "maintaining, improving, structuring, creating, and enhancing the relationship of the institution with society and selected public that financially support the institutions' mission. This interdependent view is based upon an open system in which the institutional advancement process is a form of negotiation between environmental demands and organizational needs" (p. 721).

Describing her own experience as a new development officer, Jackson captures the experience of many community college fundraisers. When she tried to emulate the practices of four-year professionals, she quickly found they weren't immediately applicable. She had to experiment to see what parts of the four-year model worked for her college and how they needed to be adapted. For example, while Jackson had little luck seeking annual fund contributions from the majority of college alumni, retirees in the community who had taken continuing education and recreational classes proved a valuable source of support (Karen Jackson, personal communication, January 2003). This indicates a fundamental difference between two- and four-year institutions and suggests why those community colleges that have had the greatest success cultivating alternative revenue sources have not adhered to any single advancement model. If there is not a single community college advancement model, there are, perhaps, some common principles.

The integration of advancement as a core function of the institution, the inclusion of advancement officers within leadership teams, and the integration of advancement and strategic planning have allowed innovative community colleges to align revenue strategies with evolving institutional visions and roles in the community. In these structural changes, community college advancement has followed the lead of four-year institutions. Institutions' capacity to cultivate private support through a calculated alignment of institutional vision with donor interest and sophisticated integrated marketing is most obviously evidenced in the escalating capital campaigns of the past two decades.

Examples of Substantive Change

At community colleges, the strategic alignment of institutional mission with the interests of external constituents as part of a comprehensive advancement process has taken very different forms. The March 2003 issue of *University Business* featured an article, "Astounding Transformations," describing the accomplishments at three community colleges. Under the leadership of Eduardo Padron, Miami-Dade College has been dramatically reengineered. Ten years ago, the college was struggling with declining enrollments, biannual budget shortfalls, and a demoralized faculty. In the past two years, enrollment has grown 12 and 17 percent. Finances have been stabilized, and faculty, facilities, and programs have been transformed. The institution's vitality and optimism has grown in concert with its advancement efforts, culminating in a $250 million campaign. According to the author, Padron approached his reengineering challenges "more like a CEO than an academic; he knew that stakeholder buy-in was crucial to the success of his efforts" (Sausner, 2003, p. 28). To stay competitive in a changing marketplace, Padron opted for more radical changes than those accomplished under a two-year plan, and instead pursued a policy of "institutionalized innovation" (p. 29).

Thanks to a radical overhaul of its mission and curriculum, Charles Stewart Mott Community College in Flint, Michigan, has seen double-digit growth in enrollments in the past five semesters and broken new ground in training in manufacturing simulation technology. Mott's success grew out of the perfect alignment of the colleges' ambitious and transformative vision and the interests of external constituents including city, state, and federal governments along with local businesses and nonprofits (Sausner, 2003). While development of the Regional Technology Center was driven by the dire economic needs of the community, President Richard Shaink seized the opportunity to radically redesign all aspects of the college's curriculum to take advantage of the new technological resources and change the culture of the institution as a whole (Sausner, 2003).

Like Mott, Capital Community College in Hartford, Connecticut, has completely revamped its academic programs and moved from an outmoded physical plant to new state-of-the-art facilities. Working with Governor John Rowland, President Ira Rubenzahl overcame substantial opposition and succeeded in moving the college to downtown Hartford as part of an urban redevelopment plan. In the process, student services have been overhauled, enhancing enrollment and retention rates. As a participant in a broader revitalization effort, Capital has also entered into partnerships with local businesses and enhanced its status as a contributor to economic redevelopment (Sausner, 2003).

Professional conferences and literature on community college advancement provide many similar examples of the way in which a willingness to pursue radical new visions has allowed community colleges to revitalize relationships with their communities and capitalize on private revenue sources. At the Dallas County Community College District Foundation, Executive Director Betheney Reid, working closely with Chancellor William Wenrich, undertook the ambitous task of developing a scholarship program to help address the county's dismal high school dropout rates. The nationally acclaimed Rising Star program guarantees Dallas County students the opportunity and financial support to earn a two-year degree if they stay in high school, graduate, demonstrate a modest level of academic potential, and have specific financial need. The program has garnered enormous private support from individuals, businesses, and other nonprofits and firmly aligned the colleges' missions with the social and economic development of the region.

In a similarly ambitious undertaking, North Arkansas College partnered with the North Arkansas Regional Medical Center to create a new nonprofit organization called the North Arkansas Partnership for Health Education (NAPHE). The college's initiative has spawned a series of partnerships with other regional organizations and national programs and now offers over 1,550 continuing education and training classes in eleven states serving 113,000 students and 1,660 businesses and agencies, garnering over half a million dollars in grants and gifts and $70,000 in revenue in 2001–2002 (Hinterthuer and Olson, 2003). North Arkansas's program has been recognized as one of forty-three Benchmark Practices for Local Economies. The Benchmark Practices program was created by Regional Technology Strategies, Inc., under the auspices of the Trans-Atlantic Technology and Training Alliance with grant support from the U.S. Department of Agriculture. The Benchmark Practices for Local Economies project identifies dynamic and effective programs at rural community colleges, focusing on demonstrable economic impact, innovation, sustainability, scale, and local support.

Southeastern Community College in North Carolina, Hibbing Community College in Minnesota, and Hagerstown Community College in Maryland were also recognized for their innovative leadership in forging partnerships and building programs that have made significant contributions to local economic revitalization efforts. These institutions' innovative technology programs grew out of ambitious strategic plans that saw a role for the college not simply as service providers but as community leaders. As their missions, partnerships, and programs evolved, the organization and business models of the schools also changed, responding to and creating new opportunities for both public and private financial support. Detailed descriptions of these and other Benchmark Programs are available on the Regional Technology Strategies' Web site (http://www.rtsinc.org/benchmark/cstudies.shtml).

Resources for Change

None of the institutions described above attempted to directly reproduce the advancement models characteristic of four-year institutions. Instead, they have looked outside their institutions, aligned their missions with the needs and interests of their communities, and reformed institutional priorities, programs, and operations accordingly. Unlike annual fund administration, campaign management, or planned giving programs, no standard model exists for undertaking such context-specific initiatives. By definition, the innovative and radical cannot be duplicated by referring to program blueprints, preferred practices, and case studies. Community colleges do, however, have access to several resources that can help them identify local opportunities and develop strategies for institutional growth and evolution.

Strategic planning models such as that outlined by Robert Sevier in his book *Strategic Planning in Higher Education* (2000) describe a process by which colleges can systematically assess external and internal environments, inventory liabilities and resources, identify opportunities and priorities, build consensus for change, and manage transition processes. While such comprehensive planning and reformation is not generally seen as an advancement function, those institutions that have most successfully adapted to changed environments have fully integrated advancement and planning (Birmingham, 2002; Glass and Jackson, 1998). Advancement functions were central to strategic planning and restructuring at Miami-Dade, Mott, and Capital Community College, as well as the colleges recognized in the Benchmark Practices for Local Economies project, which have tapped new revenue streams and created new philanthropic opportunities in the process.

At Valencia Community College in Orlando, Florida, the integration of planning and advancement functions has created an environment in which the development office can work proactively to create philanthropic and funding opportunities. The management practices and administrative procedures by which this was accomplished are usefully detailed in a Council for Resource Development paper by Hooks and Kelley (1990). Kathryn Birmingham (2002) has conducted in-depth case studies of changes in organizational structure, administrative and management activities, and faculty management activities in response to a proportional decrease in state funding at four community colleges. All of these institutions evidenced similar changes in management and administration. Organizational structures changed to identify and respond to changing market needs. The institutions became far more attentive to external constituents and greatly increased their marketing and public relations efforts. By systematically integrating advancement activities, they increased revenue from private sources and government grants. These changes correspond in part to the pattern of privatization described by Yudof and by others. By adapting to meet market demands, employing private-sector planning and marketing strategies, and partnering with local businesses and other organizations, these colleges have also reaffirmed their status as "places of public purpose."

Strategic planning has been characterized as creating a willed future. Institutionally related foundations can play a crucial role in this quest. Drawing on theories and research in public relations and fundraising, Margaret Rooney Hall (2002) argues that "community colleges have existed as open systems, drawing resources from the environment, transforming those resources, and returning them to the environment with value added so that the entire community is richer" (p. 24). This focus on relationship building provides community colleges with a solid foundation to undertake ambitious and transformative partnerships with local businesses and other community organizations. Institutionally related foundations are a privileged locus of interaction that can greatly enhance such relationships.

A brochure published by the University of Maine Foundation suggests that foundations "provide the structure and efficiency needed for the partnership between public universities and private constituencies to work" ("Private Support for Our Public University," 2003, p. 3). The vast majority of community colleges have established foundations as a vehicle for separating public and private funds and to undertake transactions that would be inefficient or illegal for a state institution to engage in, such as buying or selling real estate. Foundations can, however, make far more valuable contributions to an institution. As private nonprofit organizations operating independently of state bureaucracies and political systems, foundations can partner with local businesses and community organizations on an equal footing. Foundation trustees are typically among their most important contributors and are ideally equipped to serve as stewards, recognizing donor generosity, ensuring that donor intentions are honored and gifts used accordingly, providing fiduciary oversight of gift funds, and engaging other donors in the life of the institution.

Community college foundations also comprise an invaluable interface with the community. Trustees of four-year foundations typically represent alumni from across the nation and beyond and other leaders occupying positions of influence at a state or national level. Trustees of community college foundations also include many leaders of state and national significance. A greater proportion of two-year foundation trustees, however, represents more local constituents. Foundation boards provide opportunities for substantive and meaningful volunteer service. As Joseph Phelan observes, "Public institution governing boards are generally politically appointed, which means they are hit-or-miss in terms of donor potential. Trustees of system boards might not have an emotional attachment to any particular institution. A foundation's stature transcends advisory boards, leadership councils, and honorary societies predicated on cumulative giving levels. The foundation is an active entity with a clearly defined focus, directed energy, and measurable outcomes" (2002, pp. 48–49). Phelan demonstrates the capacity of foundations to create philanthropic potential and provides a detailed program for building or rebuilding a foundation board in *A Dynamic Foundation for Fund Raising: A Detailed Compendium for Organizing or Reorganizing for Success* (2003).

An independent foundation board can provide a long-term perspective on a college's relationships with external constituents, their shared priorities, and prospects for preferred futures. This oversight can extend beyond the tenure of many administrators and appointed college trustees and rise above momentary pressures and influences. Representing leaders of local businesses, professions, and other community organizations, they can also provide institutions with the insight and access necessary to cultivate public-private partnerships. Much as they can serve as stewards of donor interests, they can cultivate and maintain the relationships of trust essential to cooperative ventures supporting both private- and public-sector interests.

References

Birmingham, K. "Toward an Integrated System of Income Acquisition and Management: Four Community College Responses (Florida, New York, North Carolina, Texas)." Unpublished doctoral dissertation, University of Florida, 2002.

Blong, J., and Bennett, B. "Resource Development in Tough Times." *AACJC Journal,* Aug.-Sept. 1991, pp. 30–33.

Breneman, D. "For Colleges, This Is Not Just Another Recession." *Chronicle of Higher Education,* June 14, 2002, p. B7.

"Chronicle Survey of Public Opinion on Higher Education." *Chronicle of Higher Education,* May 2, 2003, p. A11.

Davies, G. "Colleges Bring Better Lives . . . But Who Will Pay?" *Chronicle of Higher Education,* May 2, 2003, p. B20.

Glass, J., and Jackson, K. "Integrating Resource Development and Institutional Planning." *Community College Journal of Research and Practice,* 1998, 22(8), 715–740.

Hall, M. "Building on Relationships: A Fundraising Approach for Community Colleges." *Community College Journal of Research and Practice,* 2002, 26, 47–60.

Hebel, S. "Unequal Impact." *Chronicle of Higher Education,* May 30, 2003a, p. A21.

Hebel, S. "Public Colleges Emphasize Research, But the Public Wants a Focus on Students." *Chronicle of Higher Education,* May 30, 2003b, p. A14.

Hinterthuer, R., and Olson, J. "Powerful Community Partnerships." Paper presented at the National Association for Staff and Organizational Development Conference, Austin, Tex., May 2003.

Hooks, W., and Kelley, S. "The Effective Linkage of Planning and Resource

Development." Resource Paper no. 43. Washington, D.C.: Council for Resource Development, 1990.

Jackson, K., and Glass, J. "Emerging Trends and Critical Issues Affecting Private Fund-Raising Among Community Colleges." *Community College Journal of Research and Practice,* 2000, 24(9), 729–744.

Kaplan, A. *2002 Voluntary Support of Education.* New York: Council for Aid to Education, 2003.

Keener, B., Carrier, S., and Meaders, S. "Resource Development in Community Colleges: A National Overview." *Community College Journal of Research and Practice,* 2002, 26(1), 7–23.

Lovett, C. "Tough Times for Colleges Demand Structural Changes. . . . " *Chronicle of Higher Education,* Oct. 18, 2002, p. B12.

National Association of College and University Business Officers. *2002 NACUBO Endowment Study,* Washington, D.C.: NACUBO, 2003.

Phelan J. *A Dynamic Foundation for Fund Raising: A Detailed Compendium for Organizing or Reorganizing for Success.* Washington, D.C.: Council for Advancement and Support of Education, 2003.

Phelan, J. "Valuable Support." *CASE Currents,* Nov.-Dec. 2002, pp. 46–51.

Potter, W. "State Lawmakers Again Cut Higher-Education Spending." *Chronicle of Higher Education,* Aug. 8, 2003, p. A22.

"Private Support for Our Public University." Orono: University of Maine Foundation, 2003. [http://www.umainefoundation.org/PDFDownloads/UMFCAT.pdf]. Accessed Oct. 9, 2003.

Sausner, R. "Astounding Transformations." *University Business,* Mar. 2003, pp. 27–31.

Selingo, J. "What Americans Think About Higher Education." *Chronicle of Higher Education,* May 2, 2003, p. A10.

Sevier, R. *Strategic Planning in Higher Education: Theory and Practice.* Washington, D.C.: Council for Advancement and Support of Education, 2000.

Worth, M. *Public College and University Development.* Washington, D.C.: Council for Advancement and Support of Education, 1985.

Worth, M. *New Strategies for Educational Fund Raising.* Westport, Conn.: American Council on Education, 2002.

Yudof, M. "Higher Tuitions: Harbinger of a Hybrid University?" *Change,* 2002, 34(2), 17–20.

Yudof, M. "The Purgatory of the Public University." *Trusteeship,* Mar.-Apr. 2003, pp. 8–12.

Zemsky, R. "Have We Lost the 'Public' in Higher Education?" *Chronicle of Higher Education,* May 30, 2003, p. B7.

DAVID BASS is director of the Council for Advancement and Support of Education (CASE) National Center for Institutionally Related Foundations.

3

A shift in the fundraising landscape has prompted community college presidents to take a more proactive approach to winning the hearts and dollars of potential donors. This chapter focuses on how college presidents and foundation CEOs can work together to gain support from funding sources.

It's Not the Race I Signed Up For, But It's the Race I'm In: The Role of Community College Presidents

J. William Wenrich, Betheny L. Reid

The title of this chapter derives from a story that might be apocryphal, but that handily serves as a parable for the changing role of the college president in fundraising, donor development, and partnership collaboration with private and public institutions. It is a story about a middle-aged Cleveland woman who, feeling out of shape, took up a regimen of jogging. After much encouragement from friends, and through gradual discipline, she bought running paraphernalia, maintained a regular exercise schedule, and increased her distances. After a time, the same friends encouraged her to enter a race. She selected a local 10K run (roughly six miles), registered, and appeared for the race on a bright Sunday morning. At the snap of the starting gun, she took off, feeling good and knowing in her heart that she would finish the race.

About halfway through any distance race, it is typical for a course to make a turnaround to the finish line, retracing the route to where the race began. So, several miles in, when no turnaround was in sight, our Cleveland woman queried a sideline official about when this turnaround would come.

"Not for ten miles," was his astounding answer. Seeing her dismayed expression, he clarified that she was running the Cleveland *Marathon,* a race of over twenty-six miles. The woman was not exactly happy about what she had learned, but even as she continued to run, she had a decision to make. Despite the odds, she decided she would try to finish the race. And she did.

Discovering what had happened, the press interviewed her the next day. Asked why she decided to try to finish the race, she replied, "It wasn't the race I wanted. It wasn't the race I trained for. It wasn't the race that I thought I was in. But it was the race! If I were going to finish the race, it was the only one available" (Trotter, 1997).

In many ways, her situation mirrors the predicament community college presidents find themselves in, especially as it relates to new expectations in fundraising and development. Private and philanthropic fundraising, partnerships with businesses, and development of college foundations were simply not in our lexicon. People wishing to become community college presidents did not enter the field expecting to raise money from those funding sources. Until recently, university programs that prepare college leaders hardly even mentioned that function as a significant role for community college presidents (Katsinas, 2003). Yet today, that role is assuming more importance for most leaders in the community college movement. We are indeed in a different race than the one we thought we entered. How did we get here?

A Need for New Funding Opportunities

The 1990s saw a surge in the growth and the reputation of community colleges across the country, yet public funding has not caught up with that surge (Davis and Wessel, 1998). During the last three years, costs continued to increase and enrollments soared, in part due to a depressed economy. By 2003, nearly every state budget had serous funding problems, and many in higher education were faced with reduced state support (Uchitelle, 2003). As a consequence, community college leaders looked for new sources of income. The increasing awareness of the impact of community colleges on the local economy allowed presidents to seek support from businesses and through individual and organizational philanthropy, building on the resource development capabilities that had evolved over the last two decades to access federal and foundation grant opportunities.

Most colleges had resource development officers who had become expert in writing grant applications for various federal program dollars. The size of college soft-money operations dependent on grants grew substantially. Federal and foundation support provided the icing on the cake for many college programs. Increasingly, colleges expanded their resource development operations to include partnerships and collaboration with private businesses, local government agencies, and other nonprofit organizations. Today, many colleges have a separate foundation in addition to their grant-writing resource-development operations. While the nature of the foundation organization, control, and polity varies widely across colleges, college presidents are increasingly dealing with foundation issues and fundraising.

In the early years of community college foundations, fundraising tended to focus on financial gifts for student scholarships, faculty chair endowments, support for program development, and the development of new facilities. Unlike their university counterparts, few community college foundations have sought to accrue endowments in support of general operations.

The new focus on external fundraising has thrust community colleges into an era of partnerships with public and private agencies for mutually beneficial outcomes. Using the Dallas County Community College District (DCCCD) as an example, we can see the progression of foundation fundraising to partnerships that are occasionally brokered by the foundations. The DCCCD Foundation's fundraising began in 1973 as a holding vessel for people who wanted to create named scholarship funds or to contribute to student scholarships in general. It expanded from that role to one of support for the chancellor and the college presidents through a group of select people known as the chancellor's council. Similar to the president's council that many colleges have, the chancellor's council consisted of individuals who annually contributed $1,000 or more for use at the chancellor's discretion, primarily for programs and recognition efforts not possible through public funding.

The DCCCD Foundation underwent a metamorphosis in the mid-1990s by becoming a broker between the business and civic community and the college district. The DCCCD Foundation committed to raising a scholarship endowment fund to create the Rising Star program. Rising Star essentially guarantees a college education to every high school graduating Dallas County senior who has at least a B average and financial need. The students are provided free tuition and books at any of the seven Dallas Community Colleges. In addition, the DCCCD Foundation became a funding conduit for new facilities that meet college needs and the interests of donors. These facilities range from a community education center on the grounds of a local hospital to a geoscience technology building on a college campus to a construction education center located near Dallas–Ft. Worth Airport. All of these facilities were funded by individuals or outside organizations.

Fundraising Roles of College Presidents and Foundation CEOs

Fundamental changes in the nature of fundraising have implications for the role of the college president. How many different hats can the president wear? Ultimate responsibility for college resources rests with the board of trustees and the president, but how much activity can be delegated to other college officials? It is our contention that the college president must be visibly in the lead because he or she represents the college in the community. Presidential commitment to fundraising, donor development, and partnerships signals that these activities are paramount for college success. Moreover, when considering a major gift, potential donors prefer to talk directly to the president. This does not, however, imply that all of the preparatory work, research, and connections are the sole responsibility of the president.

The College President. In the current milieu, the first fundraising task for a president is to identify and employ the best possible foundation executive to manage the research and legwork needed to connect with potential donors. As a visible leader of the college, the president is the person most likely to encounter those capable of giving money or establishing partnerships, and he or she must have the political and philanthropic acuity to recognize gift opportunities. Our *pounce theory* says that opportunities might occur only once in a given setting and that the institution must have the capability to recognize that opportunity and pounce on it.

Some presidents are troubled by the requirement of asking people to give money, yet they are the ones with the most opportunities to make the "ask" for large gifts. For some, this ability does not come naturally; both authors, for instance, remember the trepidation with which they first asked a potential donor for a million dollars. However, if presidents see gift solicitation as simply advocating for their colleges and telling their stories, the "ask" becomes easier. The critical part is to get potential donors to match their heartfelt interests with what the college and foundation are doing for people.

Part of the president's development of philanthropic acuity is understanding the psychological needs of and rewards for the potential donor. Frederick Buechner's (1993, p. 119) insight about vocations could apply to donor development: "Your vocation (call) is where your heart's deep gladness and the world's deep hunger meet." Fundraising is helping the donor's heartfelt gladness coincide with the deep hunger of the people you serve.

Analogous to fundraising is the president's public relations function. He or she is the media spokesperson and chief public relations figure for the college. The hands-on preparatory work for press conferences and other PR events rests with the college's public relations officer, who has the connections, the creativity, and the ability to make the public relations function work. The president, however, is still point person.

The Foundation CEO. The role of the foundation CEO is that of matchmaker. He or she bridges the needs of the college and the expectations of the community with financial resources by bringing together the right people at the right time to do the right thing. This looks easy when it is done well, but in fact it requires a great deal of research, planning, and relationship building.

Like the college president, the foundation CEO is a point person. He or she typically retains control of private and philanthropic donor development research and management, while the grant writing and management function may be handled by another individual.

The foundation CEO must understand not only the strengths, practices, and weaknesses of the potential donor, but also those of the college and its president. This knowledge minimizes the chances of a mismatch between the two parties. Research also involves understanding the marketplace and how the college can meet community objectives.

When the foundation CEO knows almost as much about the college as the college president and knows as much or more about the community, then the chances of the college securing gifts through its foundation are infinitely enhanced; the foundation CEO is now in a very proactive role of being a partner with the college president in development.

Monitoring local, state, and national trends on business and civic issues is a constant function of the foundation CEO. The obligation then is to turn over that information to the college president for action.

The foundation CEO has the moral and fiduciary responsibility to provide what was promised to the donor, and fulfilling that promise requires the full agreement and cooperation of the college and its president. It is critical, therefore, that the professional bond between the college and the foundation be seamless. Each must work with the other in full partnership to reach common objectives.

The foundation CEO is also responsible for providing timely reports to donors about the status of their gifts. Part of this reporting includes the management and investment of funds and compliance with local, state, and federal regulations. Reports should also include the results of the project. This information frequently becomes an effective managerial tool for the college president to evaluate operations of the institution.

Foundations have the benefit of a board of directors, often consisting of the community's most influential leaders with access to information, ideas, and funds. The foundation CEO must have equal professional stature of both the college president and the foundation board to command their respect and more seamlessly resolve any conflicting priorities. In the end, the role of the foundation CEO is to find the way in which the foundation, through donations, can expressly serve the college and the community at large.

The paradox about fundraising is that it isn't just about the money, it's *all* about the money. What attracts donors are the ideas: the impact a project will have, the lives it will affect, the contribution it will make. If the idea is right, the money will follow. Again, it is the role of the foundation CEO to help the college president bring the right idea to the right donor at the right time.

Many people would argue that a college president is already overburdened without adding another requirement of time to the presidential role. Our position is that fundraising is not antithetical to other presidential responsibilities. Much of it consists of viewing the other roles and daily activities from a fundraising perspective and then having qualified staff help implement the donor development and gift solicitation. If this is something the president cannot adjust to, then the president must find someone who can, because we are indeed in a different race.

References

Buechner, F. *Wishful Thinking: A Seeker's ABC.* San Francisco: Harper San Francisco, 1993.

Davis, B., and Wessel, D. *Prosperity.* New York: Random House, 1998.

Katsinas, S. *Survey on Community Colleges.* Denton: University of North Texas, 2003.

Trotter, M. "This Is Not the Race I Entered." Sermon at First United Methodist Church, San Diego, Calif., March 1997.

Uchitelle, L. "The Perils of Cutbacks in Higher Education." *New York Times,* Aug. 10, 2003, p. B4.

J. WILLIAM WENRICH is chancellor emeritus of the Dallas County Community College District, where he served as chancellor from 1990 to 2003. He has been involved in higher education for thirty-five years.

BETHENY L. REID has been executive director of the Dallas County Community College District Foundation since 1998. She has twenty-five years' experience in public affairs, marketing communications, and development.

4

*The role of the institutional trustees in supporting
foundation efforts is explored. Four priorities are
described: projecting a positive image for the college,
overseeing and maintaining an institutional structure that
supports the foundation, sustaining an engaged
administration, and encouraging innovation.*

The Role of Community College Trustees in Supporting the Foundation

Norm Nielsen, Wayne Newton, Cheryle W. Mitvalsky

With declining tax support for community colleges, creative methods of financing and fundraising are on the rise. These changes in revenue sources demand active, knowledgeable participation from institutional trustees. While not elected or appointed to be fundraisers, trustees often are called on to support fundraising efforts.

Kirkwood Community College, located in Cedar Rapids, Iowa, serves a seven-county area in eastern Iowa with a population of 400,000 and an immediate urban area of 140,000. Last year, approximately 20,000 students enrolled in college-credit classes, and another 49,000 enrolled in noncredit continuing education classes. The size of the college and scope of its mission, combined with declining tax support, makes fundraising a top priority.

The Board of Trustees at Kirkwood adheres to four principles for effectively supporting foundation efforts without neglecting other responsibilities to the college. Trustees should be aware of their responsibility to present a positive image for the college, which includes involvement at some level in college fundraising campaigns. Trustees should understand the importance of maintaining an institutional structure that supports and oversees the foundation. They should sustain a president and other college administrators who are active in the community to ensure trust between potential donors and the college. Finally, trustees should seek and support innovation from the foundation, the college, and the community.

NEW DIRECTIONS FOR COMMUNITY COLLEGES, no. 124, Winter 2003   © Wiley Periodicals, Inc.

Enhancing the Image

A primary role of the institutional trustee regarding fundraising is to maintain an environment in which the image of the college is enhanced for the members of the community. Trustees contribute to a positive image by presenting a cooperative spirit to the community; by offering visibility to various stages of fundraising; and by helping development staff and college administrators read the expressed needs, dreams, and abilities of the community.

The spirit with which institutional trustees do their work affects the community and sets the tone for the college. A board presenting a positive, cooperative, and, when possible, united front to the community helps activate potential donors. Regardless of how diligently the development staff cultivates and solicits donors, frequent split votes by the board or reports of divisiveness can negatively affect fundraising campaigns and efforts to pass or renew levies. Though healthy boards have meaningful disagreements when resolving difficult issues, institutional trustees should work toward a cohesive, team-building spirit that signals stability and trust to the community and potential donors. Longevity of institutional trustees also contributes to an enhanced image within the community. Kirkwood holds no limits on membership terms for institutional trustees as long as they are reelected. And, while the Board of Trustees has found value in retaining the same chair since 1984, new institutional trustee members who will contribute new ideas and energy are also welcomed.

Accurately reading the community's expressed needs and dreams can help institutional trustees enhance the college's image. Trustees who keep their eyes and ears open to the community can inform development staff and thus help gear fundraising efforts to the community's abilities and needs. Because of a softened local economy and stepped-up fundraising of other organizations, Kirkwood's current campaign is quieter this year, packaged in smaller bundles. Some companies currently prefer to give annually rather than commit to multiyear gifts, so we are putting a greater emphasis on annual giving efforts. Our institutional trustees, foundation board members, and development staff have been receptive to the signals from our community.

Awareness of how the board's presence, however informal, can facilitate fundraising is another important way that institutional trustees can positively affect the college's image. With each step in the fundraising process, such as identification, cultivation, solicitation, and recognition of donors, institutional trustees can contribute by being visible. Recently Kirkwood built two agricultural facilities—a swine confinement center and an equestrian center—with the help of institutional trustees who participated in identifying donors. A trustee was present at the college tours with potential donors, serving as a connector between the donors and the college. When the projects were completed, institutional trustees were present in support of donors enjoying public appreciation for their generosity.

Trustees should remember that fundraising is, first and foremost, *friendraising*. The visible presence of Kirkwood institutional trustees has been beneficial to the college, even at informal events. During Freedom Fest, a summer celebration in Cedar Rapids at which Kirkwood hosts musical events, institutional trustees intermingle with invited potential and past donors. Trustees also attend Jazz Under the Stars, a series of outdoor jazz and blues concerts co-sponsored by Kirkwood and held at various city parks. The potential influence of trustees on potential donors at these informal venues is immeasurable.

Institutional trustees also enhance the image of the college by being donors themselves. At Kirkwood, all institutional trustees and foundation board members are donors; the institution's stated goal is 100 percent participation from all college staff and faculty as well. With the prevailing philosophy that no gift is too small, all are encouraged to give within their means for the benefit of the students served by the college.

Overseeing and Supporting the Foundation

Institutional trustees should be instrumental in overseeing and maintaining an institutional structure that supports the foundation. A range of legal options is available in the relationships between the institutional trustees, the foundation, and the college. Different choices hold various strengths and weaknesses. Thomas Roha (1999) suggests that foundations that are too autonomous risk veering from their purpose, which is to serve the college. However, foundations not independent enough risk being viewed as mere legal entities of the institution.

The structure of Kirkwood Community College includes three boards that represent the seven-county area served by the college: the Board of Trustees, the Kirkwood Foundation, and the Facilities Foundation. (The Facilities Foundation oversees the use of campus vending-machine royalties for property procurement.) Although the Board of Trustees made the decision to keep the two foundations separately incorporated from the college, the foundations are not autonomous. Both are considered public and open to public scrutiny. Development staff members, who work for the Kirkwood Foundation, are paid out of the college's general fund rather than by monies raised by the foundation, to reinforce the idea that the Kirkwood Foundation and development staff answer to the college and its institutional trustees. Both foundations' board members are nominated by their own boards but approved by the Kirkwood Board of Trustees.

The college is fortunate to have an active, supportive Kirkwood Foundation board consisting of twenty-seven area leaders. The Kirkwood Foundation (hereafter "foundation") board members not only contribute financially on a personal level, but also are invaluable in assisting development staff in managing investments as well as soliciting and identifying potential donors. The foundation board members tend to be drawn from the immediate urban area, though the institutional trustees who oversee the foundation work to ensure that all of the college's constituents in the seven counties served by Kirkwood are considered in fundraising efforts.

Institutional trustees maintain visible relationships with the development staff and the foundation. The institutional trustees ratify all nominations to the foundation. Development staff and foundation members give semiannual reports to the Board of Trustees. In addition, two institutional trustees, as voting members, and the president, as an ex officio member, attend the foundation board's meetings held four times per year. The advice of the president and the institutional trustees is valued by the foundation regarding needs of the college and potential donor prospects. The presence of institutional trustees is a continual reminder of the core mission of the institution.

Because of their close working relationship with the foundation and development staff, institutional trustees understand the capacity for the development staff to contribute to the financial health of the college. The institutional trustees have been instrumental in advocating adequate development staffing for annual giving programs, large campaigns, and planned giving.

As Kirkwood's development staff has demonstrated success, the institutional trustees have hired more development personnel. Currently we have ten employees in our Resource Development Department, including three people in annual, major, and planned giving; three support staff; three grant writers; and an accounting specialist. We encourage innovative, creative thinking and results by our development staff in dealing with campaign proposals and potential donors, and we have not been disappointed.

The development staff is also instrumental in helping ensure effective communication between the institutional trustees and foundation board members. The staff organizes two social events a year at which the institutional trustees, senior administrators of the college, and the foundation board members gather to reinforce their shared commitment to the college. Foundation board members also recognize institutional trustees at every community event they organize to remind the public of the close working relationship with the institutional trustees.

While development staff members are skilled at identifying gifts that may be without charitable intent, the institutional trustees, accountable to the community, serve as another layer of checks and balances by being present and active on foundation boards. The message to the community is that the college operates at the highest code of ethics regarding the use of donations.

Sustaining an Engaged Administration

Choosing, sustaining, and standing behind an administrative staff that gets involved in the community is key priority for the institutional trustees. CEOs and other potentially large donors expect contact from the president and chief development officer. Private citizens and key leaders in business and industry need reassurance from college administrators that their donations will be used to reinforce and create educational programs, facilities, and student scholarships that truly make a difference.

At Kirkwood, the trustees encourage the president's and chief development officer's involvement in the community on bank, hospital, Chamber of Commerce, economic development, and social service boards, as well as country club memberships. Kirkwood administrators also work with other nonprofit organizations; our philosophy is that success in one campaign breeds success in other campaigns.

Development staff coordinates regular meetings on campus between Kirkwood administrators, community leaders, and private citizens. The staff plans lunches twice a month for the purpose of cultivating planned and endowed giving commitments. We invite people of the age and capacity for estate planning from throughout our seven-county area. The Kirkwood culinary arts students prepare the lunches and serve the guests and staff in the president's office, which has a panoramic view of the campus. Nearly all of our guests contribute to the college in some fashion. We anticipate future gifts totaling over $12 million because of these efforts to cultivate relationships with community members.

A high percentage of donations to Kirkwood are the result of connections made by these internal activities and through service, social, and philanthropic involvement in the community. The Board of Trustees supports the administration by ensuring enough support staff to help with its commitments. Being visible is challenging work for busy administrators; institutional trustees who understand the need for college leaders to be active outside the college will support them by maintaining the necessary support staff.

Encouraging Innovation

Fifteen years ago, Kirkwood Community College hired a new chief development officer and initiated a major fundraising campaign. No one could have predicted at the time how significantly this first campaign would galvanize various entities in the college and imprint future fundraising. Detailing the campaign will illustrate how Kirkwood institutional trustees rolled up their sleeves for an innovative fundraising effort.

Until 1990, Kirkwood's fundraising campaigns had been modest, yielding donations of $100,000 annually. With a newly hired chief development officer, the decision was made by the Board of Trustees, the president, and the foundation boards to hire a consultant to organize a large campaign effort. The consultant's preliminary interviews with nearly one hundred leaders of the community indicated a need to scale the college's $10 million wish list to $5 million and remove goals for facilities, focusing instead on student scholarships, faculty and staff development, and equipment upgrades. It was also clear that the campaign should be used to educate the public that the college was tax-assisted, not fully tax-supported. Critical issues and leadership were identified, as well as top dollar ranges to expect. Because of the interviews, community leaders were prepared for and excited about a Kirkwood campaign.

Various Kirkwood people were united for the campaign kickoff: the institutional trustees, the foundation boards, the development staff, and the president. Small organizational groups within the larger community and three hundred community volunteers were also trained for the campaign effort; each volunteer was asked to tell the Kirkwood story to five donors apiece. At the end of the two-year campaign, $6.5 million was raised—more than the initial goal of $5 million. The gain was substantial: the money had been raised; the Kirkwood story had been told many times; and relationships of trust and respect had been cemented in the community and within the college between the institutional trustees, the foundation trustees, and the development staff. Rolling up our sleeves together helped everyone appreciate each other's strengths and increased the bond of trust within the college. Before the campaign, lead gifts had been in the $50,000 range. When the campaign generated a lead gift of $1 million, institutional trustees more fully appreciated the importance and potential benefits of fundraising. They began to see more opportunities and have brought many partnerships and donors to the table since the campaign.

The institutional trustees also more fully understood the value of their geographical distribution. Because of their diverse constituents across the seven-county area served by Kirkwood, they convinced development staff that the campaign could not be one large campaign. The five rural counties had different leadership and issues from those of the two urban counties. The institutional trustees guided presentation styles in the rural counties and helped identify the key leadership there, as well as what gift levels could be expected from donors. Often, the institutional trustees accompanied development staff to county presentations. While initially the smaller counties yielded smaller gifts, estates from those smaller counties have evolved since that campaign, partially because of efforts by the institutional trustees.

With the success of the campaign, the way was paved for other innovative projects. A second large campaign was run five years later, raising $10.8 million. Smaller campaign efforts to build a swine confinement center drew a substantial $1 million—some of that funding came from sources identified by institutional trustees who accompanied development staff on visits to potential donors.

More recently, a new equestrian center has been completed. Initially planned as a $2 million educational facility, the center was upgraded to a $5 million educational and events center for horse shows on the weekends. The institutional trustees agreed to contribute $3 million, instead of the original $2 million, on the condition that the Kirkwood Foundation raise the other $2 million. This facility was built with significant funds from businesses and industries identified and cultivated by institutional trustees. The equestrian center is now completed and flourishing, with weekend bookings year-round already exceeding our projections; enrollment in the equestrian science program has also doubled.

Conclusion

An ongoing way that Kirkwood institutional trustees support fundraising efforts is simply by reminding ourselves and others of the Kirkwood story. Being clear and passionate about the mission and future of the college spreads excitement to others and helps create monetary support for the college from the community. At our institutional and foundation board meetings, we often invite students to tell their stories. All present are energized when a single mother shares how her scholarship, funded by the community, changed the direction of her life and the lives of her children. Stories like this remind us why we serve the college and increase our passion for sharing the Kirkwood story with the community. Elected or appointed institutional trustees may not see fundraising as a main priority, but it is naïve not to understand that fundraising will be a condition of trusteeship. Institutional trustees who understand their crucial role in fundraising will most effectively help the communities that they are so fortunate to serve.

Reference

Roha, T. "Touchstones of Independence." *Trusteeship*, May-June 1999, pp. 28–31.

NORM NIELSEN has served since 1985 as president of Kirkwood Community College in Cedar Rapids, Iowa.

WAYNE NEWTON has served since 1973 on the board of trustees at Kirkwood Community College and as chair of the board since 1984.

CHERYLE W. MITVALSKY, vice president of resource development, has served at Kirkwood since 1989.

5

This chapter discusses how strong, engaged presidential leadership can energize the foundation and fundraising efforts.

The Role of the President in Supporting the College's Foundation

E. Ann McGee

Not many presidents come to the position having first served as development officers. As the vice president for development at Broward Community College (Florida) for ten years, I found myself in a support role orchestrating many of the moves that the president made as we attempted to recover from a situation that found the college foundation $1 million in debt, with only $800,000 in assets. After assuming the presidency at Seminole Community College in Florida, I have spent the past seven years applying what I learned at Broward. For those who accept the challenges of fundraising, the efforts can produce results that energize not only the institution, but also the individual.

Broward Community College Experience

From the first day on the job, it was obvious that the president's role was critical to fundraising. It was on that first day that the college president, the chairman of the foundation, and I, the new development officer, visited the bank president to ask him not to foreclose on the foundation's assets. The stature of the president and the financial connections of the foundation chairman enabled the bank president to offer a stay of execution, and the three of us set about raising $1 million in three months. Our efforts were aimed at rescuing a real estate transaction gone awry and preserving the integrity of the college's foundation.

    Even though Broward Community College (BCC) could boast of having one of the oldest foundations in the country, the assets were minimal.

The reality was that the foundation board was composed of thirty men and women who had breakfast with the president four times a year, where they were also served an update on the college. In hindsight, I am convinced that they had not raised any money for the college simply because they had not been asked to do so. Raising $1 million in three months was trial by fire, a real jump start in fundraising techniques. I was invited to accompany the president and the board chairman as they made personal visits to our ten "great men." In the end, it was ten men who each contributed $100,000 toward a limited partnership, BOOK Limited, that purchased the land and Bailed Out Our Kollege.

Following the retirement of the debt, the president retired and a new president, one with former ties to the college and the community, was hired and gave his support for a complete restructuring of the foundation. The opportunities that presented themselves were to (1) set guidelines for board membership, (2) reformulate the foundation board into a working board, (3) conduct an internal and external image campaign, and (4) determine fundraising goals that would be possible for a new board to attain.

The active support of the president in these four tasks was critical. First, he initiated discussion with the board encouraging adoption of guidelines for board membership that included not only attendance at meetings but also a financial contribution. Then the president and I personally contacted all the founding board members to determine their level of interest in remaining on the board.

During these interviews, it was made clear that the new foundation board would be a group that would both actively solicit funds for the college and personally contribute. Those who indicated that they had enjoyed their time on the board but did not want to financially support the college were given the title of director emeritus. Their names were carried on the foundation letterhead but with no indication of their active service to the college. Thus the founding board members were able to leave the foundation gracefully, and a new era of active fundraising began.

The next step was to begin identifying individuals who should fill the remaining foundation board slots. A decision was made to pursue corporate CEOs so that the board would be composed of people who were capable of making sizeable contributions and who could coax similar donations from their peers. The board was viewed as selective—it was kept deliberately small at approximately thirty members—and peer pressure helped to achieve the goals that were established. The president was essential in making calls on the CEOs and convincing them that the college was a worthwhile expenditure of their time and talent.

In concert with the efforts to reformulate the board, the college conducted a media campaign designed to raise the college's image both internally and externally. Externally, people in the community would say that they liked the college but were unsure exactly what programs were offered and were unsure of the success of the college's graduates. Internally, the college employees had heard about a college foundation but had never seen it fund programs that were visible or viewed as enhancing the college's mission.

The president, along with the foundation board, established three fund-raising opportunities designed to increase the approval rating of both the internal and external constituency. With funds already on hand, the foundation began awarding mini-grants to faculty and staff. In the first year of these awards, faculty did not believe any grants would be made, thus there were few applications. Imagine the surprise when checks actually were distributed at the first faculty meeting in the fall. The next year, and every year since, applications have far exceeded the funds available.

The next challenge was to establish a goal that was worthy of the efforts of the top CEOs in the area and that would also make a difference to the institution. With BCC approaching its thirtieth anniversary, and with a unionized faculty who felt underappreciated, the decision was made to ask the foundation board to raise thirty endowed teaching chairs to celebrate the occasion.

Based on a donor contribution of $50,000 and a state match of $33,333, each endowed chair would have a corpus of $83,333, with only the interest awarded. Tenured faculty members would have to compete for the chairs, which would be awarded after a review by their peers and a presentation before the foundation board. The goal was not only to provide the faculty member with a financial incentive, but also to provide a way for the business community and donors to realize the quality of their community college faculty.

Externally, the foundation board members who comprised the Endowed Teaching Chair Committee were terrific advocates for the college as they set about raising the thirty chairs over a period of thirty months. As spokespersons for the college, they told our story better than we could. They had a passion for wanting to recognize excellence among the faculty and for putting the college foremost in the minds of the leadership of the community. The president had a specific role—that of closing the deals that board members initiated. The classic event was the personal meeting with the CEO of Blockbuster International. The meeting took five months to schedule by a board member who was a personal friend of Blockbuster's CEO. But it was the appeal by the college CEO that guaranteed the "ask" would be successful.

From a rather tenuous beginning, the Broward Community College Foundation raised over $21 million in ten years. The president's role in that success cannot be underestimated. He made himself available for visits to potential board members and to donors. He was visible in the community, taking on responsibilities from United Way to Chamber of Commerce chairmanships. His efforts, and those of the foundation board, resulted in a foundation whose assets now approach $60 million. And thanks to the involvement of one of the directors emeritus, with whom the president continued to have periodic meetings, the college received a $4.5 million gift. The scholarship bequest was matched by the state of Florida, making $9 million available for deserving students.

Seminole Community College Experience

In assuming the presidency seven years ago at Seminole Community College (SCC) in Sanford, Florida, I was struck with the realization that the trustees wanted a president who would be visible in the community. I was replacing the founding president, who had served for thirty years, and the skills the trustees emphasized in the interview were marketing and fundraising. As a 35,000-student institution located in a fairly wealthy area of central Florida, SCC had been in the shadow of a neighboring community college and had not attracted the kind of financial support that should have been readily attainable.

In some ways, the situation at SCC was reminiscent of that at Broward Community College. SCC had an existing foundation board, yet it was prevented from raising funds because its five members were all college employees. The foundation had assets approaching $1 million and no debt. However, the funds were invested in very conservative 2 percent instruments at a time when interest rates were extremely high. The foundation did not have an internal presence at the college and was only known in the community for sponsoring an annual event, the very successful Dream Auction. While this was viewed as the premiere event in the community, there was no follow-up with donors to solicit further contributions.

The situation was all too familiar. Even though I was cast in a different role—that of president and head cheerleader—I found that the challenges were the same. The foundation needed to (1) establish criteria for board membership, (2) be reconstituted into an active fundraising group, (3) implement an image campaign that would establish the college and the foundation in the minds of both college employees and the community, and (4) commit to achievable fundraising goals.

Having orchestrated the changes at Broward, I easily understood the commitment that would be required of the president. Seminole Community College needed to move into an active fundraising posture, and setting the framework that would allow that to happen was definitely the responsibility of the president.

The first step was to successfully retire the executive director of the foundation. The next step was to hire someone who, although untested at fundraising, had a great understanding of the college, accentuated by a law degree and planned giving experience. Given my original experience at fundraising, I knew that raising someone up from the ranks who had a passion for the college and knowledge of the community was the best way to jump-start our efforts. The five founding board members—who were also college employees—were offered emeritus status on the board.

With these changes in place, the foundation director and I set about soliciting new members for the board, putting a financial policy in place for investments and donations, and establishing a presence for the foundation in the community and on the campus. My joke in the early days as head cheerleader was that I had been president for 120 days and had given 120 speeches. That was not far from the truth. The community was hungry to learn about the college, and I was reluctant to turn down any opportunity to reconnect the college with the community.

Our efforts over the past seven years have been very rewarding. Thanks to Florida's generous state matching fund, we have moved the foundation's assets from $1 million to nearly $6 million. A portion of those funds, $2.5 million, has been contributed by the area's automotive dealers, with the expectation that the state match available this year will enable SCC to build a state-of-the-art automotive training facility. This effort replicates the $2.8 million in-kind donation from our construction trades community that enabled us to access $2.8 million in a facilities match from the state and build a top-notch facility for our construction apprenticeship students.

With an emphasis on faculty excellence, the foundation board launched a campaign to raise thirteen endowed teaching chairs at $100,000 each, or $60,000 per donor with an accompanying $40,000 state match. The effort was so well received that we exceeded the goal and raised $1.6 million to fund sixteen teaching chairs. The first $5,000 checks were awarded in the fall of 2003, and the presentations were made by foundation board members to surprised faculty members in front of their classes.

During the summer of 2001, the foundation board held a two-day retreat and decided that a major capital campaign was the next challenge. As the planning began, the September 11 tragedy occurred, and the economy began its downward spiral. Given the newness of the foundation and the dependence of our community on tourism and high-tech industries, the board, with the help of a consultant, decided to put the capital campaign on hold. It turned all attention to a modest living-endowment opportunity.

We decided to set our sights on soliciting one hundred champions for our cause who would make an annual contribution of at least $1,000. Designated the Presidents' Club in honor of the two presidents who had served the college, this group would provide a hundred new advocates for our cause. Their contributions would be put to immediate use to help with book scholarships, handicapped student services, car repairs, or any obstacle that might keep a student from attending the college. In return for their annual investment, the Presidents' Club members would be honored at a special dinner, recognized at the Dream Auction, and provided with access to the leadership in the community. The effort exceeded even our high expectations. In January, we celebrated with the first 114 members of the Presidents' Club and set our goal at 150 for next year.

In the description of all of these events, I hope you can see the pivotal role that belongs to the president alone. It has been said that the president is the living logo for the institution. Nothing could be truer when it comes to fundraising. People with money, power, and influence want to have ready access to the president of the college before, during, and after their contribution. They want to know that they have placed their trust and their funds into the hands of someone whom they respect, who will use their donations to further an institution in which they believe. The rewards are great for those who are willing to ask for support. It is our challenge and our duty.

E. ANN MCGEE *has served for seven years as president of Seminole Community College in Sanford, Florida.*

6

This chapter explores the role of the president as enabler and leader in promoting a foundation that is engaged with the community and responsive to the college mission.

Weaving the Foundation into the Culture of a Community College

Charles J. Carlsen

In 1967, the Johnson County (Kansas) community spoke with resounding endorsement when it approved the creation of Johnson County Community College (JCCC) by a three-to-one majority in a special countywide election. The seeds were planted for the college to become an integral part of the Johnson County community. Since its humble beginnings, JCCC has grown to enroll more than 36,000 credit and continuing education students attending classes each semester in seventeen buildings on the campus, and at more than forty off-campus sites in the community, including approximately twenty area high schools. It is the only public two-year postsecondary institution providing transfer, career, and continuing education in Johnson County.

The programs and services offered by JCCC are designed to meet the needs and interests of the community and thus to build community support. The sense of community extends beyond the campus as the college provides an extensive and broad variety of programs that address the needs of the county. At JCCC, the president reinforces and enhances the college's commitment to the community by meaningful involvement with the community. The current president is involved in activities such as Rotary, Chamber of Commerce, advisory committees in the educational and business community, and numerous other memberships and community volunteer efforts.

Having the president involved in the community benefits the college foundation in that it educates the community about the college, raises the visibility of the president in the community, and creates goodwill. These results may lead to an opportunity for the community to give back to the college and its foundation. To ensure success, the foundation should be an integral part of the college, its goals connected to the mission of the institution and to the needs of the community. In his or her interactions with the community, the college president must be sure to execute two critical approaches. A president must bring the college's mission to life and provide meaningful activities in which supporters of the college can become engaged.

Connecting the College Mission with Student Needs

The mission of Johnson County Community College focuses the college's resources on serving community needs. The greatest spokespeople for the college's mission are its students. Because of this, the JCCC Foundation features students whenever possible to breathe life into the college's mission. Students may serve as ushers at a special event, as speakers at the annual board of directors' luncheon or dinner, or as the college presence at events in the community. Students personify the mission of the college. When students speak, the audience often experiences a full range of emotion, from laughter to tears. When their stories are tied to the credibility and integrity of the president, incredible things happen, including attracting members of the community to become involved on behalf of the college. Several successful examples of engaging donors by connecting the mission of the college to student needs are described in this chapter.

Local Banker Supports Technology Center. A local banker became involved with the college as a foundation board member. During this time, he listened to numerous stories shared by students. In fact, he hired two students to work in his banks. As a successful businessman, civic leader, and chair of a local school board, he realized the importance of the community college. With his wife, he chaired the college's black-tie fundraiser and broke all fundraising records for the event. A strong relationship with the college president set the stage for even greater involvement. This foundation board member and his siblings envisioned the student who would gain from future growth of the college. When it came time for the college to build a technology center, the banker's family foundation pledged a $5 million matching grant to make sure the college's plans for the community came to fruition.

Child Development Starts Something. In JCCC's community, one couple is prominent in child development issues. Between the two of them, they chaired the local K–12 school board and the statewide Board of Regents, and they work tirelessly as advocates for child-related health causes. Their interest in supporting JCCC awoke when they heard about childcare challenges faced by students and about the early childhood education program. Over the years, their involvement with the foundation board and a strong relationship with the president led to a major gift for the college. In planning their estate, the couple set aside a cash gift of $360,000 for expansion of the campus childcare center. The new Child Development Center not only will help ease the demand for childcare in our community, but also will provide a much-needed classroom laboratory for the early childhood education program.

Goodwill Goes a Long Way. Another success story is the amazing odyssey of a couple who loved Johnson County Community College. Well into retirement, they took classes on campus and ate meals in the cafeteria. Thanks to the goodwill they received from staff and students, including the assistance they had locating their car in the parking lot, the couple found their way to the president's office to say that they would like to do something for the college. Although this couple had not been treated differently from many other couples who take classes on our campus, they wished to donate $1 million to the college foundation—and an additional $700,000 on settlement of their estate. The president, along with the leadership of the foundation, was pivotal in establishing trust that this couple's donation would impact the lives of students for many years to come.

Gala Dinner Honors Supporters. In 1987, the president, along with a few of the community's civic leaders, envisioned and launched a scholarship fundraising event. The idea of a black-tie event honoring the Johnson Countian of the Year—centered around a multicourse banquet served between dance sets of big band music—was perceived by the skeptics as a real stretch. But despite this initial criticism, the gala now has some of the most sought-after tickets in the Kansas City area, becoming more prosperous every year. The highlight of the evening is a scholarship recipient's story. The student stands in front of six hundred or more corporate sponsors and guests and shares a story of how a scholarship helped him or her overcome adversity. A hush falls over the ballroom as the story unfolds. In this moment, the college's mission is brought to life for those in the room, with an assist from volunteers on the gala committee, the foundation, and the college itself. Over the years, the gala has generated $2.2 million for scholarship endowment. Last year, the total foundation endowment of $7,848,452, plus donations from corporations, private foundations, and individuals, allowed JCCC to provide $965,854 in financial assistance to approximately 600 students, or an average award of $1,600. These awards were in addition to grants, loans, work study, and money given to students from other funding sources.

Engaging Supporters in Meaningful Activities

Volunteers are the lifeblood of any organization. The college is no exception. Johnson County Community College—through its advisory committees, service organizations, and foundation—employs the services of over four hundred community members throughout the course of the year. In fact, civic engagement and responsibility is identified as one of the college's strategic goals. Many of its 2,465 full- and part-time employees serve in various volunteer capacities, with the blessings of the college. The foundation treats its volunteers with utmost respect for their time and talents. In the end, these volunteer relationships have resulted in some very successful results for JCCC students.

Engaging External Stakeholders. As evidenced by the number of outstanding business and civic leaders (116) serving on the foundation board, engaging external stakeholders has been a priority of the president. These leaders reinforce current initiatives and launch new ones to generate higher levels of volunteerism and contribution that will benefit students. That said, these board members build the bridge to civic, community, and workforce participation and partnerships throughout the metropolitan area. The college is in a unique position geographically because it serves and engages constituents on both sides of the state line. The president serves on numerous boards such as the Greater Kansas City Chamber and the Kansas City Catalyst, as well as hospital boards in both states. This leadership not only engages external stakeholders but also educates them about the college. In this venue, the president speaks to and illustrates the "invisible need" in Johnson County for scholarships (approximately one in five of our students receives some type of aid for tuition). This interaction with external stakeholders has been an ongoing priority with the president during his tenure. It strengthens ties with new and ongoing donors as the college pursues new levels of excellence through high quality and consistent fundraising activities. The role of the president is to promote the mission of the foundation—promoting access to the college and advancing institutional excellence through financial support. The guiding principles of the foundation—lifelong learning, teaching, and culture—are avenues to engagement of the external stakeholders.

Engaging Internal Stakeholders. Faculty and staff participation in foundation activities is led by the president as he encourages support throughout the campus. Ultimately, the object is a shared purpose and sense of community as faculty and staff work toward their own goals and have fun in the process. The Dollars for Scholars Auction, a benefit for student scholarship and programming, is an example of this involvement by faculty and staff. Twenty-five teams representing over twenty college programs and scholarship funds conduct gift solicitations across the entire county. Dollars for Scholars is a night of fun marked by the enthusiasm of five hundred attendees, with over two hundred primarily faculty and staff volunteers. The event builds a bridge from the campus to the community, as its faculty and staff volunteers get their families and friends involved. Word spreads about the college and its need for scholarship dollars. A few years ago, the president provided the leadership needed for the event to become a campuswide affair, involving teams from a diverse group of departments.

The foundation celebrates employee contributions with an annual employee block party, a celebration with the president at which a commemorative block engraved with the year is presented to every employee who contributes to the foundation. The president proudly displays his blocks in his office. Faculty involvement is also encouraged by inviting the faculty association president to foundation board activities and inviting faculty to present to the foundation executive board.

The President Leads, and Major Gifts Follow

The president's role in the community to create and maintain a culture where outreach, collegiality, trust, and relationships are emphasized naturally leads to major gifts. This involvement inspires members of the foundation board, faculty, staff, and students to be effective goodwill ambassadors. This community connection has made the foundation successful enough that foundation members are no longer recruited. Now community members ask to be considered for board openings.

The role of the president is crucial to the success of the foundation. Internal and external leadership sets the tone for fundraising activities. Involvement in the community creates many opportunities to build the bridge that will ultimately benefit students in pursuit of education at JCCC. The president leads by example and celebrates the successes that will make a difference in the lives of others.

CHARLES J. CARLSEN *is president of Johnson County Community College in Overland Park, Kansas.*

7

*This chapter focuses on successful practices in
fundraising through contractual, partnership, and
entrepreneurial activities by community colleges.*

Generating New Sources of Revenue

Tony Zeiss

The effects of a weak economy have presented community college leaders
with the serious challenge of discovering alternative revenue sources while
maintaining their fundamental missions. It is clear that community colleges,
described by Davis and Wessel (1998, p. 5) as "the great American aid sta-
tions of higher education," are facing a permanent shift from being public-
supported to being public-assisted institutions. To varying degrees,
America's community, junior, and technical colleges have responded to
budget cuts by reducing costs, becoming more efficient, and prioritizing
which classes and services are offered. Most colleges have also initiated
activities to augment revenues. Increased lobbying for local, state, and federal funds has been one immediate response to recent budget cuts, but
sources of additional private funds have been slower to develop. America's
community colleges must learn to become educational enterprises.

Educational Enterprises

Community colleges can become entrepreneurial in many ways. Most colleges already solicit funds through their foundations and provide contract
training for business and industry. Others have developed successful partnerships for raising increased public and private grants. A few pioneers in
fundraising have developed the capacity to generate revenue through a
fee-for-service organization. As time passes and the need increases, our
colleges will discover new avenues for becoming more self-supported.
Each college should examine every revenue source and pursue all methods for raising funds that are most closely aligned with its mission and
meet its needs.

NEW DIRECTIONS FOR COMMUNITY COLLEGES, no. 124, Winter 2003 © Wiley Periodicals, Inc.

Becoming an entrepreneurial organization is exciting to some presidents and trustees, frightening to others. Yet the current economic state of community colleges and the increasing demands for their services compel them to become more enterprising. Critics of this notion will suggest that instructional quality will be adversely affected. Others may suggest that becoming entrepreneurial will in some way cause a drift in the college's mission. In reality, these colleges will more fully validate their missions and values by becoming more self-supported. They won't sacrifice instructional quality by becoming entrepreneurial; rather, they will ensure instructional quality by raising the additional funds necessary for an effective teaching and learning environment (Zeiss, 2002).

Community colleges share a basic mission to help students achieve their educational goals. As colleges expand their services to include new populations in the adult sector, delivery methods may change dramatically, but the fundamental mission remains the same. A student is a student whether she or he is the traditional emerging worker, an existing worker, a transitional worker, an entrepreneurial worker, or someone who is pursuing hobby interests. Community colleges have long cherished the core values of accessibility, responsiveness, and teaching and learning excellence. By strategically meeting a growing demand for corporate training and providing convenient, lifelong educational opportunities for adults, community colleges will be revalidating their core values with expanded markets.

There is also the argument that if a college begins raising significant funds on its own, the decrease in public funding will be accelerated. This reasoning raises the question of whether it is better to wait until the well runs dry before digging another. It is logical to assume that as community colleges become more self-supported, they will ultimately be better positioned to serve their communities and their students more consistently and with higher-quality services.

There is a huge and growing worldwide market for educational services. Workers and employers are spending large amounts of money on retraining to acquire skills needed for existing or better jobs. Zane Tarence (2002) estimates this market, minus military training, to be an immense $735 billion annually. People understand that their earnings are directly connected to their educational credentials, and employers understand the necessity of having knowledgeable and skilled workers in order to be competitive. Community colleges hold enviable positions in their communities to take advantage of this emerging market of students and would be wise to expand their services to include it. Tarence states, "Nationally, community colleges have the opportunity to be the Wal-Mart of high-quality, well-defined educational services, and no other market player has the ingredients to compete in this space if institutional leaders engage wisely, with authority and creativity" (2002, p. 2). Further, for-fee education providers such as the University of Phoenix, DeVry, ITT Educational Services, and others are moving quickly to roll out impressive national expansion models in order to capture a share of this education and training market (Tarence, 2002). There are two overwhelming reasons for colleges to strategically pursue this market with zeal: survival and the need to capture a sizable market share before the proprietary colleges do.

Of course, there are multiple benefits for community colleges that transform into dynamic educational enterprises; they will establish an alternative source of revenue, receive greater respect and value from their communities, and become much more customer-focused and efficient organizations. Fortunately, there are some wonderful examples of the entrepreneurial spirit in colleges throughout the country. Many colleges are successful in garnering contractual training for companies and public agencies; others are known best for partnering with companies or community-based organizations, and a few have become leaders in other entrepreneurial activities. Astute presidents and trustees will develop a strategy for learning about successful entrepreneurial practices and implement them at their colleges.

Contracted Services

Successful examples of contracting with an organization for education and training services have been presented in literature and at conferences, and a few colleges have become leaders in this area. Typically, they have built solid relationships with their clients over the years, beginning perhaps with a small training contract for teaching leadership, supervisory skills, or the latest computer applications skills. Over time, the client begins to understand that the college can train and retrain its employees faster, better, and cheaper than anyone else, including the client. The college's contracts generally increase dramatically when the organization's key officers come to this realization.

It is important to understand that these evolutionary relationships don't happen by accident. The college must learn to sell, train, and service the client well. The most successful colleges have sales teams, proposal writers, excellent trainers, and a strategic plan for making the enterprise successful. The good news is that colleges do not have to invent a successful contract-training program. There are sterling models for marketing and servicing contractual training. The community college counterparts in Great Britain experienced severe cuts in public funding over a decade ago, and they have become experts in contract training.

Humber Institute of Technology and Advanced Learning in Toronto is known around the globe for its contract training. For the last thirty-five years, this enterprising college also has developed a market for educating students in developing countries. Humber recently contracted with the Malaysian government to offer fast-track three-year degree programs leading to four-year degrees through Penn State University. The college's faculty and staff travel to Malaysia to screen and orient students who then attend Humber College, usually majoring in mechanical engineering.

Humber has built residence halls for its international students and provides comprehensive support services to ensure student success. After completing the three-year degree in two years, the students transfer to Penn State to finish their baccalaureate degrees.

Humber also contracts with Ningbo University (China) to teach Chinese students there for the first two years. These students then attend Humber for their third year and transfer back to Ningbo University for their fourth year. The students usually major in international business. Humber Institute of Technology and Advanced Learning is now raising about $7.5 million annually by recruiting international students. In 2003 the school is serving 668 foreign students.

In 1995, several German-owned companies in the Charlotte, North Carolina, region requested that the college develop a German apprenticeship program to train their new employees. These six companies wanted proven training systems similar to those in their home country. Central Piedmont Community College trainers worked with the companies to develop the curriculum and the delivery system customized to their corporate partners' specifications. The companies paid for all student expenses of the program, including books, tuition, and fees, and provided each student with one day off from work each week to attend classes.

The Center for Business and Technology (CBT) at Johnson County Community College in Overland Park, Kansas, provides public and private organizations the opportunity to develop their supervisory strength through its Supervisory Assessment Center. Organizations contract for a service that involves a full day of assessment activities, including videotaped role-playing segments. After evaluation, individual development and training plans are prescribed and provided. Recently, a large teaching hospital used the center to assess all forty-two of its managers and supervisors. This remarkable partnership allowed the hospital to economize on its professional-development budget by targeting training objectives that had been validated by the center. The college is able to grow its CBT through contracts with outside organizations.

Business Partnerships

Another very successful method for raising revenue is to partner with a business for mutual benefit. Many partnerships have been distinctly fashioned to meet the needs of the collaborating organizations. And many result in increased dollars, equipment, or facilities for the college and free customized training for the other organization. Labor-intensive businesses, for example, recognize that community colleges often can fill their staff development needs more efficiently than any other training provider.

Some partnerships involve a joint delivery of training or related services to third parties. For example, hundreds of colleges are partnering with Microsoft, Cisco Systems, and other software firms to provide regional computer certification training. The colleges have already established credibility in their communities as quality service providers, and commercial interests recognize the advantage of partnering with these colleges to reduce costs and advance the growth of their training business.

Bellevue Community College (Washington) has become the national leader in the development of an information technology (IT) curriculum. Through its partnerships with Microsoft, the National Science Foundation, the American Association of Community Colleges, and the League for Innovation, Bellevue has established nationally validated and internationally recognized skill standards for IT workers, developed nationally respected IT training services for community college faculty, and played a pivotal role in responding to the nation's pressing need for cybersecurity training. The college has garnered over $3 million for these initiatives.

Johnson County Community College (Kansas) partnered with the Burlington Northern Santa Fe Railroad to provide customized training for its employees. The railroad was so impressed with the college's responsiveness that it built a training facility on the Johnson County campus.

Delta College in University City, Michigan, was a pioneer in corporate partnerships. In the 1980s, Delta partnered with the General Motors (GM) Corporation to develop and operate GM certification training for service technicians throughout the country. The GM-Delta Automotive Service Educational Program has long been recognized as a model community college–corporate relationship.

San Diego Community College District has established a corporate council to help the college more effectively serve its corporate partners and develop new revenue streams. The council has twenty-one members, who pay an annual membership of $5,000. In the eighteen months of the council's existence, the college has received $560,000 in donated equipment and supplies. The purpose of the council is to keep the college informed about industry trends and workforce needs. This partnership between the college and the corporate community has provided a much-needed communication link and new revenues.

Enterprising Illinois Central Community College has partnered with the Caterpillar Corporation to develop customized training for Caterpillar's employees. Corporate employees worked with college professionals to develop the curriculum for training dealer-service technicians. Caterpillar built a training center on the Illinois Central campus, donated the latest equipment, and provided the necessary support to ensure a successful training program.

Entrepreneurial Activities

A most provocative opportunity to increase revenues lies in the area of entrepreneurial activities, with community colleges becoming especially creative and innovative. Several colleges are following the university model of creating 501(c)(3) corporations to allow them to enter the lucrative arena of private enterprise. It is important that a college's board of trustees endorses such activities and that an appropriate team of innovators and salespersons is placed in charge of this effort. These activities often are out-of-the-box initiatives, and many of them may not be successful. Colleges generally have some latent entrepreneurs who are just waiting for the chance to be creative and start their own small business. The employees who contribute to this endeavor must be encouraged to be innovative and should be rewarded for their efforts.

Many community colleges have created university centers on their campuses to produce lease revenue and provide expanded services to their students. Other colleges have established restaurants, coffee shops, and bookstore complexes that attract nonstudents. Some colleges have created comprehensive exercise facilities that encourage public memberships. A few colleges are funding innovations in online learning, videos, and other products to be sold on the world market. A real opportunity exists for these colleges to leverage their reputations as expert education and training providers into the learning stores of their communities. By using the inherent talent of their own faculty and staff, and by contracting with community experts who need a marketing agency, community colleges are well positioned to be successful.

Seattle Community College has pushed the envelope by establishing a corporation to operate a private, for-profit call center. The center handles financial credit-related services. It works with lenders to reduce interest rates for its clients, with net profits directed to the college. In its first year of operation, the college received approximately $1 million in income.

Lane Community College in Eugene, Oregon, has developed a management program in cooperation with regional United Way Agency directors. Although the program is nonprofit, it is entrepreneurial because Lane had to develop saleable services to fund the activity and to keep it funded. The college's Business Development Center offers vital learning to area nonprofit organizations. This program features twenty content-rich workshops and ten two-hour individual coaching sessions to help build sustainable nonprofit organizations. The college intends to market the modularized training to create additional revenue for program stability. Fees, donations, and a grant currently fund the program.

An Enterprising College Model

Central Piedmont Community College (CPCC) in Charlotte, North Carolina, has been positioning itself as an enterprising organization for decades. This innovative college of six campuses and 70,000 students measures its success on the value it brings to its students and its community. Recognizing that quality services cannot be rendered with public money alone, CPCC has focused on becoming expert at contracting training, partnering with various entities, and developing entrepreneurial opportunities. The college was recently recognized by the National Alliance of Business as the 2002–03 Community College of the Year. CPCC was selected by the General Accounting Office, the Jobs for the Future study commissioned by the Ford Foundation, and MGT, Inc., as a national model for its innovative efforts to meet workforce training needs in the Charlotte region. In 2002, the college was invited to join the prestigious Newcomen Society of the United States in honor of its consistent performance in becoming a national leader in workforce development.

Contracted Services. Central Piedmont Community College is living up to its vision to become the nation's leader in workforce development, especially through contract training. This enterprising college has become the preferred outsource training provider to many Charlotte-area businesses. Family Dollar Stores, a growing national discount clothing store chain, is headquartered in the college's service area. The college worked with corporate training personnel to establish job profiles of Family Dollar Store positions. College trainers then developed pre-test and post-test activities and prescriptive training modules for existing and new employees. The college is preparing a train-the-trainer program to be delivered to select community colleges across the country, to serve the needs of 4,500 Family Dollar Stores. This relationship has had tremendous benefits to the corporation and to the college. The founder of Family Dollar Store recently donated several million dollars to establish a scholarship fund for CPCC.

Several years ago, CPCC began contracting with the Charlotte Douglas International Airport to provide workplace literacy classes. Building on the success of those classes, the airport has expanded its education and training services through the college's Corporate and Continuing Education division. CPCC now trains law enforcement officers, professional staff, and frontline airport workers in a variety of occupational areas. Command Spanish, leadership and management courses, and computer application skills are currently the most popular courses. The college prices its training services in a competitive fashion determined by local market rates.

Business Partnerships. Central Piedmont Community College has developed an extraordinary partnership with Duke Energy. This visionary company wishes to expand and diversify its technical employee base. The college and employees of Duke Energy are developing a Global Technical Workforce Development Initiative. The project's strategy is to recruit English as a Second Language students for technical training. Initial training will include electrical and electronics technology and electrical and electronics engineering technology. These certificate-based programs will also lead to an associate's degree. Duke Energy has donated $50,000 to the development of the program and is inviting other industries to become involved in the initiative to help promote Charlotte's technical learning community.

Many community colleges have become deeply involved in teacher education as the shortage of teachers across the nation has become a serious problem. Maricopa Community College of Phoenix has been a leader in this activity, and a new association called the National Association of Community College Teacher Education Programs has been established. CPCC has partnered with the local school district to provide the certification classes for teaching assistants and lateral entry teachers. Lateral entry teachers already possess a baccalaureate degree or higher, but lack the educational certification required to teach. CPCC offers these courses using both classroom and online instruction. The college and the University of North Carolina at Charlotte have developed a two-plus-two program for emerging teachers, and CPCC plans to initiate similar programs with two private universities.

The Alliance for Employee Growth and Development is a ten-year partnership among three local telecommunication companies and CPCC for industry-specific training. Courses vary according to the alliance's needs, but currently include computer certifications, punctuation and grammar, medical coding, Microsoft Office 2000, and keyboard skills.

The Pathways to Employment program at CPCC is its most celebrated partnership. The college partnered with its local Workforce Investment Act Board, the Department of Social Services, the Chamber of Commerce, the State Employment and Security Commission, and local businesses to establish a nationally recognized welfare-to-work program. The college has now produced ten classes of graduates, with a 77 percent retention rate, an 81 percent employment rate after six months, and an average hourly wage of $10.50. During a visit to Charlotte in 2002, President George W. Bush lauded the program as a commendable welfare-to-work program for the United States.

Entrepreneurial Activities. The faculty and staff of Central Piedmont Community College recognized that the college's greatest asset was its people and their ability to be creative and provide products and services. They also recognized that there was a growing need for education-related services and products by nonstudents. For example, the requests for career services and career testing by nonstudents have grown tremendously. The need for video-based ESL programs has increased throughout the country. Additionally, community colleges across the nation need better access to leadership training, as veteran administrators are retiring in droves.

To capture these and other business opportunities, CPCC established a separate 501(c)(3) organization that encourages faculty and staff to submit proposals. A committee reviews proposals, and if they are accepted, the appropriate seed money is provided to develop the service or product. Employees often are given a reduced workload during this stage of development and are provided the assistance of the organization to help refine, test market, and package the product or service. Once the product or service is marketed and revenue is created, the innovator receives a percentage of the net profit. A slightly higher percentage of the net profit benefits his or her department, and the remaining profit stays within the corporation to fund new small businesses or to help the college in other areas of need. In effect, the college has created a small-business incubator that provides start-up capital and professional nurturing to get the businesses established. Some examples of current or planned businesses include an ESL videotape series, online leadership and teacher education certification classes, education and workforce development research services, career counseling services, leasing services, a college press, and a soon-to-be-built conference center. The residual benefits are numerous. This activity is generating great interest among faculty and staff and has become a fine activity for professional renewal. The entrepreneurial spirit is invigorating for people, and the college has established another source of revenue. CPCC has also expanded its influence in the community by providing new education-related services to new populations.

Implications

Community colleges are involved in a funding transformation from being publicly supported to becoming publicly assisted organizations. This fundamental and permanent change will ultimately create better, more efficient, and more market-sensitive colleges, although the learning curve will be steep and painful. It is hoped that colleges that embrace the opportunity to seek new avenues of revenue will find that doing so affords them additional flexibility as well as rewarding them with greater control over their own destinies. Their faculty and staff will find a more stimulating work environment, and their students will benefit from a college that understands the importance of being customer focused.

Community colleges have an exciting opportunity to reinvent themselves while staying true to their core values of accessibility, responsiveness, and excellence in teaching and learning. The entrepreneurial spirit of these colleges will guide them through the transformation of becoming educational enterprises, with contracted services, business partnerships, and entrepreneurial activities in this new era.

References

Davis, B., and Wessel, D. *Prosperity*. New York: Times Business, 1998.

Tarence, Z. "A View from the Outside In: Community Colleges as Entrepreneurial Community Learning Centers." *Leadership Abstracts,* Nov. 2002, 15(11). [http://www.league.org/publication/abstracts/leadership/labs1102.html]. Accessed Oct. 21, 2003.

Zeiss, T. "Show Me the Money." *Trustee Quarterly,* Association for Community College Trustees, Fall 2002, pp. 27–29.

TONY ZEISS *is president of Central Piedmont Community College in Charlotte, North Carolina.*

8

When a grants development office is perceived as an integral component of a community college, it can effectively raise significant amounts of public and private funding to advance the institutional mission, vision, and strategic plan.

Grants Development in Community Colleges

Neil Herbkersman, Karla Hibbert-Jones

Constrained by economic pressures, community college faculty, staff, and administrators must seek external funding to support their projects and ongoing programs. Thus an institutional grants office and foundation have emerged as essential components of effective community colleges. These twin resource development functions can successfully focus efforts to advance the institutional mission, vision, and strategic plan.

Even with shrinking federal and state funding for discretionary grants, significant amounts of public funds are available. This fact compels most community colleges to invest in a grants office to manage the grants development process. Bauer (1995, p. 10) states, "The role of the grants office is to assist the organization to meet the present needs and to prepare for future needs by securing external funds that will move the organization toward its goals." However, to be successful, community college grants development offices require an organizational commitment, strategic organizational structures, clearly defined roles and processes, and top performing personnel. This chapter provides examples from the Grants Development Office (http://www.sinclair.edu/departments/grants) at Sinclair Community College (Dayton, Ohio), including a major joint public-private fundraising initiative.

Organizational Commitment

The organizational commitment for the grants office begins with the community college leadership. There should be board- and executive-level agreement that grants development is an institutional priority. This commitment

63

must involve the active participation of the college leadership as well. For example, at Sinclair Community College, the leadership is actively involved in all aspects of grants development: developing an annual grants agenda; participating in go/no-go decision making for individual projects; obtaining off-campus partners; planning projects; reviewing, editing, approving, and signing proposals; and presenting proposals to funding entities.

Organizational commitment is also indicated by where the grants office and the foundation office are located within the organizational structure of a community college. Clearly, there are different organizational reporting models, and each has advantages and disadvantages. Many colleges have adopted an *advancement model,* with the grants office, the foundation, the public information office, marketing, and publications all in one division reporting to a chief advancement officer. The main advantage of this model is the synergy developed through close working relationships among these externally focused organizational units. The organizational model at Sinclair includes the foundation, a separate 501(c)(3) nonprofit organization reporting to the president, and the grants office, which functions on a university-sponsored *research model* (as described by Beasley and others, 1982) within the administrative division. This reporting structure has proven to be effective, resulting in significant public and private funds raised to support the college.

Regardless of the organizational reporting model, to ensure maximum institutional impact, the college strategic plan should be the underpinning of all institutional development efforts—both for the grants development office and for the foundation. Clearly, this can be difficult to do, especially in larger institutions with hundreds of faculty and staff who are passionate about writing proposals to support projects and programs that may be only marginally aligned with the college's strategic plan.

Strategic Organizational Structures

The organizational structure of the college influences the roles played by the grants office and foundation personnel, and the institution's priorities steer the fundraising activities. Grants development offices should document their processes and clearly define the roles of key players.

Clearly Defined Roles of Grants and Foundation Offices. In colleges where the grants and foundation offices are separate departments, it is critical that each clearly defines, communicates, and coordinates roles. For example, at Sinclair, where the two development functions are separate, there is an operational agreement for the foundation to manage the fundraising for initiatives that do not require budgets, such as scholarships, gifts, and general contributions. The grants office manages the fundraising for projects that require budgets and uses the standard approval process for private and public funding sources. If the grants office identifies a local foundation as a possible funding source, there are discussions with the Sinclair

Foundation director. This ensures that both offices do not solicit funds from a local foundation unless multiple proposals are acceptable. Because the grants and foundation offices have the same overall goal of raising funds and have high levels of communication and coordination, Sinclair can create synergistic public-private partnerships.

Fundraising Objectives Based on Institutional Priorities. It is essential that the grants and foundation offices closely align their fundraising with institutional priorities. Fundraising objectives for the Sinclair Community College Foundation are set by a volunteer board made up of the college president, the treasurer, members of Sinclair's Board of Trustees, faculty, and community members. Fundraising objectives for the grants office are based on an annual agenda developed through interviews with the president, the provost, the chief operating officer, vice presidents, deans, directors, chairs, and current project directors. Goals from divisional business plans are also incorporated into the grants agenda. For each new major project, the grants development personnel, project director, business office, and grants accounting office analyze the opportunity with a decision matrix. The decision matrix helps determine project alignment with institutional goals and answers the question, "Is Sinclair prepared to win the grant?" (See Appendix to Chapter 8 for a copy of the decision matrix.)

Documented Processes of the Grants Development Office. Community college faculty and staff are busy individuals who often are not experienced in developing grant proposals. A well-documented grants development process can increase faculty and staff understanding of and interest in proposal development. Grants offices should thus develop tools and techniques to streamline the grants development process, including the following:

- Templates of word processor and spreadsheet files for common grant application sections (college description, evaluation methods, budgets, and so on) that may be easily adapted and adopted
- Sample funded proposals on the departmental website
- Access to commercial Web-based grants databases to automate grants funding research
- Faculty proposal-writing workshops and periodic proposal-writing tips e-mailed to key proposal developers.

As part of a process improvement, the Sinclair grants office analyzed the grants development flowchart to identify the longest chain of dependent steps in the process. Goldratt (1997) calls this the *critical chain*. Using Goldratt's Theory of Constraints project management assumptions, the grants office analyzed the critical chain for any bottlenecks in the process, identifying the proposal-writing phase as the major system constraint. Sinclair's grants office personnel can write several proposals concurrently but prefer not to engage in multitasking on projects of institutional significance.

They write all proposals that have institutional priority and assist faculty and staff with proposals at the departmental level.

In response to the constraint, the grants office built time buffers into the critical chain at the proposal-writing phase. Time buffers are created by relieving the principal author on the grants office staff of all other responsibilities for the duration of the writing phase. This allows the principal author to focus maximum effort on writing to avoid multitasking, considered by Goldratt to be a time waster. Sinclair grants office personnel write one significant proposal at a time to reduce mistakes and rework and eliminate delays along the critical path. The writing task is completed faster, and the proposal is completed earlier. Another example of a time buffer used to address writing constraints is having faculty, staff, and external consultants write proposals.

Roles of Key Players Within the Grants Development Process

There are multiple roles in the grants development process, and it is important to identify individual players.

Project Champion. Every project must have a champion—usually the originator or owner of the project. He or she often becomes the project director or a principal investigator.

Executive Leaders. Executive-level staff involvement in prioritizing and supporting grants projects is necessary. At Sinclair, the president, provost, and vice presidents review and approve all grant projects to ensure they advance the mission, vision, and strategic plan.

Financial Team. The financial team helps identify auditable matching funds, analyzes the return on investment for new projects, ensures fiscal accountability and stewardship, calculates indirect cost rates, and provides post-award financial management.

Support Team. Administrative support staff in many departments facilitate communication, organize meetings, and assist with the internal transmittal process and final production of proposals. Staff in institutional research might provide resources to document the need for projects, while information technology staff help plan and support new initiatives and public information staff publicize new projects and their success stories.

External Partners. Partnerships with other educational institutions, nonprofits, and governmental organizations often are needed to shape and meet project goals. Businesses and industries often are sought as partners to strengthen the development, implementation, and evaluation of projects.

Consultants. Internal and external consultants can be used throughout the grants development process to provide content expertise, review, and editing of proposal drafts.

Roles of the Grants Development Office

The grants office is the catalyst and prime mover of the grants development process. Grants office personnel play the following essential roles.

Researcher. Grants offices perform two distinct research roles: documenting the need for projects and locating funding sources. Early in the proposal-development process, grants developers conduct research to assess and document a compelling need for the proposed project. Most proposals require a well-documented description of the project's significance, including internal and external data sources such as key informants, case studies, statistical analyses, and surveys (Bauer, 1999). Using commercially available databases of funding opportunities, Web pages, and printed newsletters, grants office personnel research potential funding sources, agency regulations, and the needs and interests of potential funders.

Facilitator. The grants office communicates with and appropriately involves individuals who will be affected by the grant project, sometimes elevating the original idea into a more meaningful project for the college. The grants office establishes the agenda for and facilitates a series of project-planning meetings, building consensus for the project scope and details.

Dreamer and Realist. The grants office helps college supporters envision and plan strategic projects that do not exist, while balancing decisions against resource realities and constraints. For example, the college might be unable to meet proposal deadlines or might lack resources such as personnel, space, or matching funds to commit to a project.

Planner. After deciding to pursue a funding opportunity, grants developers create a master plan with a timeline detailing each step of the development process and its strategies and key players. Working with the project champion and other key players, the grants office facilitates planning for the entire project, including the goal, objectives, activities, timeline, budget, evaluation, and management plans appropriate for the project. Planning is a crucial precursor to the writing of the proposal.

Writer and Editor. As indicated, the grants office at Sinclair writes all proposals of institutional significance and assists faculty and staff with proposals at the departmental level. Such assistance may be in the form of editing or formatting, ensuring that the final written document is compliant with the agency's request for proposals (RFP) and uses proper grammar and spelling. If the RFP permits, it is important to include in the finished product well-designed diagrams and graphics to help reviewers understand major points. Good document design, a critical skill in the grants office, includes the use of clear prose and graphics that work together as an integrated whole (Schriver, 1997).

Budget Developer. The grants office helps the project director identify the resources necessary to achieve the project objectives, ensuring that budgets are realistic, make efficient use of existing resources, and are based on standard operating procedures of the college.

Evaluation Expert. Grants development personnel help project directors create sound formative and summative evaluation methods that match the complexity of the proposed project.

Archivist. The grants office maintains records on proposal submissions, grant status, award amounts, and other details to document the return on investment and impact on the college. Legal requirements specify that funded proposals be archived, and it is a good practice to maintain source documents and data sources used in proposals.

Cheerleader. Because grants development can be a long and demanding process, it is important to help the development team stay focused and remain energized on their joint goal of creating a competitive proposal.

Finisher. The grants office secures required signatures, packages the proposal for electronic submission or hard-copy shipping, and sends it before the deadline.

Competencies Required Within the Grants Development Office

Because of the competitive nature of proposal writing, the superior performance of grants personnel with well-developed competencies enables the college to compete successfully for external funding. Professional development activities help grants development personnel attain higher-level competencies. Spencer and Spencer (1993) indicate that competencies are like icebergs, with both visible (above the waterline) and hidden (below the waterline) components. The visible or technical competencies are the required skills and knowledge for a specific job such as planning, project management, and communication. The hidden or behavioral competencies, such as a strong customer-service or teamwork orientation, allow top performers to complete tasks and achieve objectives. Superior performers exhibit higher-level behaviors of both technical and behavioral competencies and, in general, use more competencies, frequently achieving better results.

Technical Competencies. The Council for Resource Development, an affiliate of the American Association of Community Colleges, conducted a job analysis to identify the knowledge and skills needed by resource development officers in community colleges. The job analysis identified 31 broad areas of responsibility and 240 discrete tasks in addition to an extensive list of knowledge and skills. Planning, facilitation of planning, and group facilitation were among the most critical knowledge and skill areas identified. Effective communication is also a prime technical competency in the grants development office (Brumbach, 1992).

Project-Planning and Management Techniques. The most critical phase of any project is planning (Kerzner, 1998). An estimated 80 percent of the time involved in a proposal is invested in project planning; the final 20 percent focuses on writing and editing a proposal. Grants office personnel must be highly effective in facilitating small-group project planning. The Sinclair grants office has adopted Compression Planning with Storyboarding (McNellis, 2003) to streamline project planning and focus thinking. Whatever the project-planning process used, successful grants offices should become skilled in leading project-planning meetings.

Each proposal outlines a project plan with a need, a goal, objectives, activities, an explanation of project management, and evaluation methods, thus knowledge of project planning and management are essential. Good project-planning and management techniques are also needed for success in high-volume grants offices to coordinate and complete multiple projects simultaneously. Control techniques such as workflow schedules (Gantt charts, bar charts, or milestone charts) and work breakdown structures (Program Evaluation and Review Techniques or Arrow Diagram Methods) are necessary planning tools for meeting tight deadlines in highly competitive environments (Kerzner, 1998). To be most effective, the grants office personnel should have a working knowledge of project management methods.

Effective Communication Strategies. Before grants are approved for submission, the grants office personnel must communicate with college leadership about the proposals under development, explaining how the proposals advance the strategic plan and fit the organizational mission. Effective communications are crucial to roles played during the grants development process. Once a proposal is funded, the grants office must communicate with the grants accounting function to hand off strategic management information such as proposals, budgets, award letters, and contracts. Communication between the grants office and the community college foundation is essential as well to ensure integration of the fundraising effort. All communication must be timely, brief, and accurate. The Sinclair grants office relies on e-mail communications and a highly developed Web page to provide information to internal and external customers.

Behavioral Competencies. Examples of behavioral competencies considered to be critical in the Sinclair grants office are customer service and integrity.

Customer Service. A successful grants office provides a high level of service to its customers, the faculty, staff, and administration. Gitomer (1998) points out that loyal customers will proactively refer other people for services. By providing professional, knowledgeable, and reliable service, the grants office will develop faculty and staff loyalty and commitment to work on future projects. A successful grants office providing high levels of customer service need not actively recruit faculty to work on proposals. The faculty will proactively seek the grants office for assistance.

High Integrity. The reputation of the community college is at stake, and there are legal issues related to the successful management of public funding. The grants office must ensure that the proposals submitted contain factual information, the budgets do not supplant institutional funding, and the matching funds are legitimate and auditable. College executives do not want to read articles in local newspapers about malfeasance or misuse of public funds on one of their grants.

Professional Development for Grants Office Personnel

Resource development staff should be trained, top performers. Grants development is a high-stakes game, and community college development personnel should be well-trained leaders, project planners, and resource managers with high ethical standards and extensive knowledge of community college philosophy, processes, student needs, and pedagogy. Successful grants and foundation office personnel are expert planners, facilitators, communicators, and technology users. Resource development personnel require knowledge of donor motives and giving methods, budget and financial matters, tax laws, research, technical and contract writing, and document design.

Professional development for grants and foundation personnel is found in books, journals and periodicals, benchmarking visits with other colleges, and training through professional organizations such as the Council for Resource Development (http://www.crdnet.org). The Council for Resource Development provides a range of professional development opportunities and technical assistance for community college presidents, chief development officers, grants personnel, and foundation trustees and personnel.

An Example of Joint Public and Private Development

Sinclair Community College was selected by a local task force to manage a countywide initiative for providing alternative education environments and social services to an estimated 5,000 to 6,000 area high school students who had dropped out of school. To provide overall vision, daily management, and program oversight, Sinclair created a new department called the Fast Forward Center. The center is a public-private partnership providing a comprehensive, systemic infrastructure to serve youths who have dropped out of high school. The five-year, nearly $20 million project requires the active collaboration of four major Dayton-area partners: a local corporate foundation, the Montgomery County (Ohio) administration, Sinclair Community College, and Miami University Middletown and its Applied Research Center. The Fast Forward Center develops, maintains, and evaluates a continuum of alternative high schools and academic support programs for out-of-school youth.

The chief executive officer of a Fortune 500 company and member of Sinclair's Board of Trustees agreed to serve as the private fundraising chair for the initiative. The foundation of the Fortune 500 company is coordinating the overall fundraising from local private and corporate donors. Foundation personnel create the case statement, make the lists of potential donors, schedule the visits, and solicit funds from private donors. Montgomery County is contributing $2.5 million and is allocating additional block grants to the initiative; Sinclair's president and the county administrators leveraged earmark grants from the U.S. Department of Labor Employment and Training Administration and from the Ohio legislature. The final partner is the Applied Research Center of Miami University Middletown, which is under contract for a five-year longitudinal study of the Sinclair Fast Forward Center program and the alternative schools. The Sinclair grants development office was instrumental in obtaining the Applied Research Center as a partner, in helping create the evaluation strategy for the out-of-school initiative, and in subcontracting for services.

In agreeing to manage the overall initiative, Sinclair's president committed the institution's two fundraising departments to perform major roles in the project. The Sinclair Community College Foundation cooperates with the corporate foundation to create the case statement documents and to consult on all private fundraising efforts. It also serves as the depository and steward of all private funds.

The Sinclair grants development office develops and writes the proposals to public agencies, including a major earmark grant to the U.S. Department of Labor. Since the college serves as the fiscal agent for the Fast Forward Center, a significant amount of grants office personnel time is required to collaborate with the Business Operations Division in order to manage the subcontracting with alternative high schools and other providers. The subcontracting requires ongoing discussions with partners, funding agencies, and legal counsel. Annual contracts must be renegotiated and subcontracts revised and signed. The grants office also provides technical assistance to the Fast Forward Center director and staff. Technical assistance includes developing and revising project budgets, forecasting income and expenses, and developing strategic plans for public fundraising.

Clearly, the Fast Forward Center provides an example of how a community college can assume the major administrative role to address a significant local problem. The twin fundraising departments—the grants development office and the foundation—can effectively and efficiently work together and with other organizations to advance the community college agenda.

With a strong organizational commitment, strategic organizational structures, and clearly defined roles and processes, resource development offices at community colleges can raise significant funds to advance the mission, vision, and strategic plan. Colleges that invest resources in their grants and foundation offices receive a significant return on investment measured not only by the amount of dollars raised, but also by the outcomes of the funded projects and programs that advance the institution. Advancements to the college, divisions, or departments; increased student success; improved faculty performance; and meaningful contributions to the community are realized through external funding secured through strategic development processes.

References

Bauer, D. *Administering Grants, Contracts, and Funds.* Phoenix, Ariz.: Oryx Press, 1995.

Bauer, D. *The "How To" Grants Manual: Successful Grantseeking Techniques for Obtaining Public and Private Grants.* Phoenix, Ariz.: American Council on Education and Oryx Press, 1999.

Beasley, K., and others. *The Administration of Sponsored Programs.* San Francisco: Jossey-Bass, 1982.

Brumbach, M. *Chief Resource Development Officer: A Job Analysis for the National Council for Resource Development.* Washington, D.C.: National Council for Resource Development, 1992.

Gitomer, J. *Customer Satisfaction Is Worthless—Customer Loyalty Is Priceless.* Austin, Tex: Bard Press, 1998.

Goldratt, E. *Critical Chain.* Great Barrington, Mass.: North River Press, 1997.

Kerzner, H. *Project Management: A Systems Approach to Planning, Scheduling, and Controlling.* New York: Van Nostrand Reinhold, 1998.

McNellis, J. *Compression Planning.* New Brighton, Penn.: McNellis, 2003.

Schriver, K. *Dynamics in Document Design.* New York: Wiley, 1997.

Spencer, L., and Spencer, S. *Competence at Work: Models for Superior Performance.* New York: Wiley, 1993.

NEIL HERBKERSMAN is director of grants development at Sinclair Community College, Dayton, Ohio.

KARLA HIBBERT-JONES is assistant director of grants development at Sinclair Community College, Dayton, Ohio.

Appendix to Chapter 8

GRANTS DEVELOPMENT DECISION-MAKING MATRIX

Project Agency and Title: _____

Decision: ☐ Bid ☐ No

Bid Factors	Negative (0 1 2 3)	Neutral (4 5 6)	Positive (7 8 9 10)	Estimated Rating
1. FIT WITH COLLEGE MISSION, STRATEGIC PLAN, RESEARCH FINDINGS	Does not align with the College mission and plan	Marginally matches the College mission and plan	Helps fulfill the College mission and plan	
2. BACKGROUND (Expertise of College in project area)	Weak in area or totally new area to College	Average experience in this area	Strong experience in this area	
3. PROPOSED COLLEGE PRINCIPAL INVESTIGATORS	Poor in-house team with few available known new hires	Good in-house team, with good available new hires	Superb in-house team, with superb known new hires	
4. FINANCIAL POTENTIAL (Return on investment)	Poor short term, poor long term, likely to cost College	Questionable long-term, questionable short-term	Excellent long term and short term, likely to yield a margin	
5. TEAM MEMBERS (College's partners and major subcontractors)	Partners and subcontractors dilute/weaken effort	Partners and subcontractors have no major effect	Partners and subcontractors have enhancing effect	
6. ADVANCE INFORMATION ON RFP (Adequate information to respond)	Did not expect RFP, unprepared	Generally up-to-date with RFP, no major negatives	Good favorable information, ready to respond	
7. COMPETITIVE ASSESSMENT (Competition and funding probabilities)	Competition is very strong, odds are under 10%.	Open competition, odds are 10-50%	Open competition, odds exceed 50%	
8. CAPABILITY TO EFFECTIVELY RESPOND	Do not have staff time to adequately respond	Stresses staff time, but are able to respond	Have staff time to develop highly competitive proposal	
9. FUNDING AGENCY CONTACT, HISTORY, AND RAPPORT	College is unknown to this agency and staff	College is known to agency and staff	College has well-developed working relationships	
10. COLLEGE RESOURCES (Space, personnel, matching funds)	Requires significant investment of college resources	Requires marginal investment of college resources	Requires minimal investment of college resources	

Total Score (Sum of scores for each factor evaluated)

Involved alumni are alumni who will give, and then ask how they can do more. If a college knows how to cultivate and engage its alumni, it is well on the way to financial health and growth.

Keeping in Touch: Alumni Development in Community Colleges

Mark J. Pastorella

Community colleges are particularly and favorably positioned to obtain support from their alumni. Alumni recognize the value they received as students. Most live in the vicinity of the college and take dual pride in knowing that their gift in support of the community college is also an investment in their community. Many community college students had a life-altering experience at the college (such as being influenced by a professor who helped them to determine their life and career goals) or were offered access to education when no other access was available. Those who achieve success often will reflect on the community college's importance in shaping their lives, and their resulting gratitude will stimulate support.

Alumni are the largest single constituency affiliated with the Monroe Community College (MCC) Foundation (see Chapter One for additional discussion of the MCC Foundation). Our alumni serve as mentors, ambassadors, donors, board members, and as an invaluable resource for our student body. Gratitude and appreciation underscore the efforts of alumni. Alumni serve and give because they received an extraordinary value—a high-quality educational experience at an affordable price—and because they personally benefited from the college's commitment to accessibility. With proper planning, alumni can serve as a powerful resource for the college.

Alumni and the MCC Foundation

Established in 1982, the MCC Foundation has developed more extensive alumni programming and fundraising initiatives during the most recent decade. To date, over 3,000 MCC alumni have contributed to the foundation in excess of $3 million. In the mid-1990s, the foundation successfully completed its first capital campaign, titled "Creating a Legacy," which raised $6.5 million. The campaign's largest gift from an individual was a $1 million contribution from an alumnus.

Currently, 25 percent of the MCC Foundation board of directors are alumni. Each director consistently supports the annual fund at leadership levels and plays an integral role in major gift solicitation. Within the board organization, an alumni council is actively engaged, which adds alumni representation and perspective to its many activities. As our alumni age and reach their peak giving and planned giving potential, we anticipate total alumni giving to be the fastest growing donor segment.

The MCC Foundation directors and staff make a significant effort to engage and involve alumni through events such as the Scholarship Open, the Gold Star Gala, and the Salute to Excellence. The Scholarship Open, our annual golf tournament, creates scholarships and raised $50,000 in 2003. The Gold Star Gala dinner features a one-of-a-kind auction with items donated by college faculty and staff and in 2003 raised $46,000. The Salute to Excellence is the MCCF signature event, a dinner to honor those demonstrating extraordinary generosity in support of the college and to recognize the outstanding accomplishments of four graduates by inducting them into the Alumni Hall of Fame. Alumni are invited to each event, serve on the planning committees, and set and achieve fundraising objectives.

With over 300,000 alumni, the foundation finds it necessary to use a profile to determine which alumni are to receive invitations to special events, although donors and past event attendees always receive invitations. Like most special events, our planning process has a relatively short time frame, and the successful completion of the event provides the sense of satisfaction and purpose that keeps volunteers motivated. Even so, our volunteers regularly change, and turnover on event-planning committees is encouraged to continue adding new life to the event. Volunteers are recruited to serve on committees based on their interest, as measured by questionnaires, and on a particular strength the volunteer could bring to the event. The highlight of the Salute to Excellence, the MCC Alumni Hall of Fame induction, recognizes the professional and community service of alumni as well as their service in support of the college.

Additionally, the MCC Foundation presents Alumni Weekend and many small events organized and attended by alumni. Alumni Weekend started as a small, targeted annual dinner, built momentum, and now regularly attracts hundreds of alumni. The Alumni Weekend event has evolved over the last five years and is attended almost primarily by alumni. The event is a friendraiser; ticket sales cover the event's cost, and the goal is to bring alumni back to campus. All fundraising studies relating to alumni giving have shown a significant increase in the giving rate among alumni who have been recently engaged or on campus. Alumni Weekend kicks off with a large event: dinner on campus on Friday night. Students provide musical entertainment and sing the alma mater, and alumni get the opportunity to see the many changes to our campus and to reunite with former professors and classmates. Saturday's events have included class-specific reunions, athletic competitions, chicken barbecues targeting alumni with families, and a special alumni dinner to recognize the Athletic Department's Alumni Hall of Fame inductees.

Alumni volunteers have introduced a new Welcome Day event through which alumni are invited back to campus on the opening days of each semester to greet new students. The Alumni Council, a subcommittee of the MCC Foundation board, developed the idea based on the common student experience of confusion and fear of coming to a large campus on the first day of the new semester. The event was conceived and launched in conjunction with the Admissions Department and the Campus Center Staff. Alumni volunteers are trained and positioned throughout the college and at campus entrances to assist students with common first-day questions and directions.

Finally, alumni are offered a variety of services and benefits, most notably the use of college facilities, career services, a dynamic alumni website, and subscriptions to the MCC Foundation newsletter. All alumni services help to build, maintain, and strengthen relationships with alumni and stimulate support.

Steps to Success

Recognizing that there is great diversity among community colleges nationwide, I offer the following areas to focus on for programs looking to grow.

Find Affluent, Influential Alumni. There is little that cannot be accomplished with the leadership of a small group of affluent and influential people. Consider identifying alumni who fit this mold, perhaps through an alumni recognition program or event. Targeting this group of people highlights the accomplishments of your college and builds its prestige and image. The success of alumni is a shared success, as the college played a significant role in their career paths. With direction and purpose, a small group can begin to direct effective alumni giving and programming initiatives. The most significant concept of the alumni group should be inclusion with the development office and the college. The Alumni Council is an official subcommittee of the MCC Foundation board, and the chair of the Alumni Council serves on the MCC Foundation Executive Committee.

Increase the Visibility of Alumni on Your Campus. On the first days of school, at major student events, and at commencement, we have alumni volunteers visibly interacting with students. They dress in college attire and show alumni spirit. Identify college employees who are alumni, and enlist their support as well. The seed is planted when students witness alumni returning to campus, often leading graduating student leaders to express interest in alumni programming.

Develop a Successful Annual Fund. Your alumni expect to give, but you have to ask. Consider using direct mail and telemarketing to motivate alumni to become donors. Acquisition can be expensive in the short term, but the long-term value of alumni support is worth the investment. Seek major gifts from prominent annual fund supporters. Your annual fund supporters have identified themselves as being connected to the college. By involving the donor in the aforementioned activities, you can develop the connection and often find the opportunity to supplement donors' giving with special giving opportunities (such as capital campaign or deferred giving).

Achieve Excellence. Take a personal approach to alumni planning. Build and foster relationships, and the alumni program will grow to become a significant part of the college community. Learn about your alumni and specifically about their student experiences—who was their favorite professor, what clubs and organizations were they involved in, what was their program of study, and how did they feel about their experience? Use this information to build, strengthen, and grow the alumni connection, and soon your fundraising and event attendance will exceed expectations.

Have Realistic Expectations. In the beginning, do not expect extraordinarily large participation rates. Large four-year colleges such as UCLA receive gifts from only 15 percent of alumni, and all alumni programs face difficulty in attracting alumni to events. Community colleges are new to alumni programming compared with other colleges with extraordinarily successful alumni programs. At MCC, the first graduating class—the Class of 1964—contained seventy-two students, most of whom are currently in their late fifties and early sixties. With time, more and more of our alumni will reach their peak giving and planned giving years, and increased support will follow. Alumni donors should be tracked as often as possible; with each gift and each contact, an effort should be made to grow the connection and to gain additional information.

Know Your Mission. Having a mission and knowing what your alumni can do to help is critical in community college alumni programming. At MCC, the purpose is to connect alumni to the college, with the belief that connected alumni are more likely to support the foundation. Four-year residential colleges attempt to bring alumni back to campus at annual social events such as homecomings and reunions, but community college contact with alumni can be much more frequent and engaging. Engaged alumni give, then ask what more they can do to support the alumni program and the college. To keep their interest and spirit alive, having a definite mission is a must.

Moving Forward

Private institutions established hundreds of years ago already know that alumni are a significant resource for advocacy, ambassadorship, and financial support. The task of developing effective community college alumni relations does not rest solely with development and alumni professionals; it requires a collegewide effort with a significant emphasis on faculty involvement. A strong development and alumni-relations program is an extraordinary asset to any college.

Mark J. Pastorella is director of alumni and planned giving at Monroe Community College Foundation in Rochester, New York.

10

Not so long ago, the word "fundraising" scarcely made an appearance in the community college lexicon. Along came worldwide social, technological, and economic upheavals. Welcome to the future and the new realities of community college advancement.

Feels Like the Third Wave: The Rise of Fundraising in the Community College

Mark David Milliron, Gerardo E. de los Santos, Boo Browning

Alvin and Heidi Toffler's careers are built on exploring and engaging future trends, challenging community, business, and education leaders to wrestle with broad-based changes that often shape the very foundation of our economies, social institutions, and belief structures (Toffler, 1989; http://www.toffler.com). More recently, they focus their efforts on their concept of the *third wave:* our economic and societal transition from the agrarian age (first wave) to the industrial age (second wave) to the information age. While the first- and second-wave trends are dominated by farming and factories, respectively, the third wave is characterized by the move to a knowledge- and service-based economy dominated by rapid change, technology, and globalization. Their core argument is that the third wave is driving transformative change, even while prior waves continue to play out locally and globally. For example, we may be waxing prophetic about third-wave disruptive innovations such as the Internet (Christensen, 1997; Tapscott, 1998), yet people in third-world communities still struggle with agrarian-age issues of raising crops and storing water. We note with some humor that many in education have little problem understanding these three waves and their concomitant states, as many of our institutions still operate within industrial factory models on agrarian calendars meeting the needs of the information age. Nonetheless, these sweeping conceptual frameworks help inform our dialogues about what lies ahead for our work in education.

NEW DIRECTIONS FOR COMMUNITY COLLEGES, no. 124, Winter 2003 © Wiley Periodicals, Inc.

As we approached this volume on fundraising in the community college in this transformational context, conducted our background research, exchanged dialogue in focus groups as part of ongoing trend research (Milliron and de los Santos, forthcoming), and previewed the chapters submitted, we began to feel as if fundraising might be a major part of our own third wave in the community college movement. As we delve into the institutionwide impact, the external constituency issues, and the transformational strategies surrounding fundraising, we are increasingly convinced that this is not simply a discrete trend. Fundraising is part and parcel of a wave forming, foaming, and frothing, already flooding across the community college movement. It has clear implications for how we teach, reach, and lead and will likely lead to heated dialogues about our mission and vision in the communities we serve.

Of course, by presenting this argument we are not contending that the community college movement is distinct from the larger waves Toffler outlines. Indeed, it is quite the opposite. Community colleges and their precursors have long ridden these societal trend waves, morphing and moving to meet the needs of our larger communities. What we are arguing is that from the microcosm of the community college movement, fundraising may be an integral part of the third in a series of profound transformational waves that have driven and are driving change in our work. The first wave was centered on *comprehensive integration* and the rise of the comprehensive community college movement itself. The second wave surrounds *entrepreneurial expansion,* as community colleges moved into a host of strategic entrepreneurial, social, and educational collaborations, including a predominant focus on workforce development and technology. The third wave is about *institutional advancement,* entering into full partnerships on the economic and educational landscape and developing the relationships necessary to support our institutions more fully on the road ahead. Indeed, the true test of an advanced relationship may be what we are willing to ask from it.

Comprehensive Integration and the First Wave

As most in the community college field know, the swells that would lead to the emergence of the first wave in the community college movement were seen with the emergence of Joliet Junior College in 1901 and the subsequent flow of academically focused two-year junior colleges. Soon thereafter arose a tide of technical institutes and colleges focused on providing practical and technical training that led to work for returning soldiers and a legion of others hoping to take full advantage of all the industrial revolution had to offer.

But it wasn't until the 1947 report "Higher Education for an American Democracy"—commonly known as the Truman Commission Report—that an explicit call rose up for the creation of community colleges (Zook, 1947). Comprehensive community colleges were to blend the best technical and vocational education with the more traditional junior college education in an effort to more completely open higher education to all citizens, not just the wealthy. It was an idea whose time had come; however, it wasn't until the passage of the 1965 Higher Education Act and its subsequent amendments in 1972, coupled with a new set of soldiers who began returning from a new war in the 1960s and 1970s ready to use the G.I. Bill, that the true embrace of the first wave began to take hold.

Indeed, until this time the American Association of Junior Colleges was rife with conflict between private and public institutions and rarely focused on technical schools as serious partners. Soon after the comprehensive integration wave hit, however, the association changed its name and became the American Association of Community and Junior Colleges. In addition, during this time, most private junior colleges took a number of routes out of the business of two-year education, either becoming four-year colleges or converting to public institutions. Still others just closed their doors or merged with other institutions (Roueche and Schultz, 1966).

The League for Innovation in the Community College came into being during this time frame and can arguably be called a child of the first wave. In the mid-1960s, when B. Lamar Johnson, a professor of higher education at the University of California–Los Angeles, came forward with the idea for the League, one of the core missions of the organization was to reach out to the cadre of emerging comprehensive community colleges and provide models for teaching and learning practices, leadership strategies, and administrative protocols (O'Banion, 1985, 1988; http://www.league.org).

Of course, the major challenge of the first wave was thoughtfully integrating technical-vocational and academic education process, practice, and values. And as we will demonstrate with each of the community college waves, there were broad-based and discrete steps needed to significantly transform (1) internal operations, (2) external relations, and (3) best-practice adoption to truly take advantage of the transformation at hand.

Internally, the host of two-year colleges in transformation began to do the hard work of exploring curricular integration of technical-vocational programs and aligning them with the general education requirements necessary for college transfer programs. Moreover, as degree, diploma, and certificate programs were built to be a "ladder" and allow for smoother progression in different career areas, faculty and staff were challenged to work together in new ways and to truly value other modes and motives for learning. Jacobs (1993) went as far as asking the question in his article titled "Vocational and General Education: New Relationship or Shotgun Marriage?" As the article notes, many of these internal transitions were and *are* messy. Indeed, lest we think the first wave is completely finished, a number of institutions still wrestle with building bridges between the often segregated worlds of technical-vocational education and two-year liberal arts and general education programs (Bailey, 2002).

While many major internal transformations from the first wave continue—particularly the sticky organizational culture issues—the major *external* relations elements also clearly define this wave. As our institu-tions—many still juggling a multitude of monikers including *college, com-munity college, technical college, technical institute, junior college,* and *community and technical college*—began to reach out and communicate their new roles and goals, they were met with an external public that had yet to truly grasp what a community college was. In many communities, an institution that added *community college* to its name perhaps fifteen years ago often is still labeled a tech college or institute in public debate and dialogue. Legacies linger. It was even a challenge for high school counselors to embrace the full scope of community colleges, so much so that the College Board designed a section of its website aimed directly at these professionals to dispel myths and outline opportunities afforded by community colleges (College Board, 2003). Even today, many people, including some who are leaders in creating educational policy, are shocked to learn all that a comprehensive community college can offer.

Finally, another major challenge of the first wave was documenting, disseminating, and *adopting best practices* in truly integrated, comprehen-sive community college programs on both the internal and external level. The League for Innovation in the Community College and the American Association of Community Colleges are but two of the many nonprofit asso-ciations and organizations that take the lead in providing resources to col-leges in this regard. And even though the integrated community college mission is clearly the national norm and is being patterned internationally in Canada, Europe, Australia, and Southeast Asia (Kintzer, 1998), the trans-formation brought on by the first wave is still ongoing in many parts of the country. For good examples of this we can look to the newly formed Kentucky Community and Technical College System (http://www.kctcs.edu) or track the move by the Louisiana Technical and Community College System to more closely align and fully accredit its more than forty techni-cal education sites statewide (http://www.lctcs.net).

As with all the waves, to truly make the most of the positive change afforded, college leaders have to be able to address the internal and exter-nal issues while adopting new best practices. For example, with a combined approach in the first wave, institutions may be well prepared to offer com-prehensive programs, but their communities may be unaware of what is available. Moreover, they may advertise seamless programming, but in fact have a batch of internal bureaucratic hurdles that tarnish the experience of new students. Finally, there may be a willingness within the internal com-munity and external community to accept the new roles and goals; how-ever, without best-practice models and information, many colleges are left hard pressed to make the transition or meet their communities' dynamic learning needs.

Even though there were and are challenges in truly embracing the first wave, much like Toffler's waves, the move toward *comprehensive integration* became a center of gravity for the community college movement for years.

Fundraising in this context tended to be dominated by strategies to maximize public support through federal, state, and local funding streams—what many in higher education finance call "hard money." Hard money is recurring and more stable revenue—often formula-driven and tax-based monies—to support the educational mission of our institutions. In addition, aggressive grant-writing departments where charged with obtaining government and foundation grants to subsidize standard programs and services—often called the search for "soft money." Soft money is nonrecurring grant income intended to support curriculum development or retention initiatives, for example. The quest for the right mix of hard and soft money in this respect was what college CEOs and trustees were most focused on when fundraising came up in discussion. That is, until they began to move into the second wave.

Entrepreneurial Expansion and the Second Wave

Beginning in the 1970s and truly emerging in force in the 1980s, community colleges began to embrace a bold set of *entrepreneurial expansions,* most prominently in the areas of workforce development. We can in part track the emergence of this trend by looking at League for Innovation programs. For example, the League has a history reaching back to 1968 of showcasing key corporate relationships formed by community colleges with business and industry. In 1985, however, the League hosted an appropriately titled event called "We Mean Business: Policies for Partnerships in Industry and Education" in Kansas City, Missouri. The conference was hosted in partnership with the Kansas City Regional Council for Higher Education, and Johnson County Community College served as the local host. This was the beginning of a major dialogue on community colleges creating systemic programs and services to meet the needs of business and industry. One of the more controversial topics of this forum surrounded the issue of offering discrete contract training in addition to traditional vocational, technical, or academic programs in order to dynamically meet workforce needs. Traditional academics maintained that for-profit training by a college was heretical and that deep connections with local businesses were compromising to the values of higher education.

Based on this meeting, the League formed the Business and Industry Services Network (BISNET) and formally created an initiative to explore workforce development as a major role in community colleges. In 1992, the BISNET leaders held a business and industry services workshop, followed in 1993 with a conference on total quality management. Clearly, business and industry training as a significant role for community colleges was a blossoming debate. The League then formed the Community College Business and Industry Alliance, which brought together community college leaders and top companies such as IBM, Kodak, and Xerox. The Alliance helped lead a series of regional forums on business and industry training. And in 1994, the League hosted its first Workforce 2000 conference, at which 600 attendees were expected but 1,200 registered.

The concept of workforce development as a core mission outside of discrete vocational and technical programs, particularly in noncredit programs, heated up. Some talked of the emergence of the "shadow college" and the driving need to bring these often-derided operations into the light and induce a redesign of community college programs and services to meet the changing workforce needs of the United States (Warford, 2000–01). Others began advocating for the closer connections with business and industry as a means to introduce "quality" into our curriculum programs (Baker and others, 1995; Bober, 1991; Spanbauer, 1992). Key authors and leaders began noting the central role community colleges were playing in the transition to Toffler's third-wave information-age economy (Davis and Wessel, 1998; Gates, 1998; Tapscott, 2000).

For example, Federal Reserve Chairman Alan Greenspan noted in his September 2000 testimony to the Committee on Education and the Workforce of the U.S. House of Representatives that community colleges were becoming an essential element of the U.S. economy, particularly because of their emerging workforce focus: "This process of stretching toward our human intellectual capacity is not likely to end any time soon. Indeed, the dramatic increase in the demand for on-the-job technical training and the major expansion of the role of our community colleges in teaching the skills required to address our newer technologies are persuasive evidence that the pressures for increased learning are ongoing" (Greenspan, 2000).

At the time of Greenspan's speech, community colleges were already being looked to in efforts to meet workforce needs. For example, beginning with the continuous quality movement and continuing on as the dot-com economy heated up, community colleges were seen as major drivers of economic growth. From helping run Motorola University through the Maricopa Community Colleges in Arizona to providing just-in-time training to the Burlington Northern Santa Fe Railroad employees at Johnson County Community College in Kansas, they quickly ramped up a host of vital industry-certification programs. Next, they developed new programs in the information technology arena (such as Cisco Network Academies and Microsoft IT Academies) and developed mechanisms to keep their fingers on the pulse of emerging technology needs (Milliron and Miles, 2000; Perez and Copenhaver, 1998).

In addition to the demand for information technology, the need for K–12 teachers, nurses, biotechnology workers, and homeland security personnel has more recently driven the community college workforce focus. Community colleges are designing fast-track programs to transfer teacher candidates to local universities, developing programs for alternative teacher certification, and offering staff-development opportunities for existing teachers (Boggs and Bragg, 1999; Education Commission of the States, 2002; National

Association of Community College Teacher Education Programs, 2002). They are also playing a critical role in recruiting, retaining, supporting, and graduating nurses. Nationally, associate degree nursing graduates are highly successful on a registered nurse exam and are in high demand as transfer students to bachelor of science in nursing (BSN) programs. Closely related to the allied health programs that support nursing are the emerging biotechnology programs at community colleges nationwide. These programs are laying the groundwork to provide the workforce necessary to fuel the biotechnology boom predicted for the next decade.

In short, when it comes to meeting workforce needs that impact the economy—such as the development of flexible, fast-track, and high-quality programs—local, state, and national entities increasingly turn to community colleges. The value of community colleges to the American economy has become so great that the international community is looking to the United States to model these open-access institutions that are considered the engines of the middle class (Davis and Wessel, 1998). And, as in the first wave, entrepreneurial expansion led to broad-based internal and external transformations and the search for best practices.

There is little doubt this transformation has led to serious and often painful *internal* transitions as many institutions wrestle with the best way in which to organize their colleges to more flexibly meet the workforce needs and the resulting entrepreneurial expansion (Nielsen, Baird, Browning, and Milliron, 2003). Indeed, up to the late 1980s, very few colleges had anything resembling a vice president for workforce development. Now it is absolutely a common position. A more vexing problem than hiring a person and changing a title, however, has been how to blend this expansion into the first wave of comprehensive integration. How do we mix credit and noncredit programs? How do we create more modular and less traditional programs to meet worker and industry needs? How do we maintain our academic standards and not sell out? How do we leverage new technology, online learning, and enterprise resource-planning and customer-relationship management tools (Milliron, 2001)? These and a crush of other very good questions have been and continue to be wrestled with as this second wave of entrepreneurial expansion floods through our business.

Helping with these internal challenges in the second wave have been the learning-centered education advocates (Barr and Tagg, 1995; Boggs, 1996; O'Banion, 1997; O'Banion and Milliron, 2001; Wilson, 2002). We argue that the explosion of learning-centered education initiatives has been an understandable and welcome result of the waves of demanded reforms and ever-changing missions thrust upon education. Learning-centered education helped colleges center their efforts and avoid the "irrational exuberance" that often accompanies the explosion of new technology and workforce rhetoric (Milliron and Johnson, 2002; http://www.league.org/league/projects/lcp/index.htm).

As community colleges address these internal changes, they also are again communicating to their *external* constituencies and noting their role as workforce engines. And even though this transformation came quickly on the heels of the first wave, it added to our value proposition, as our institutions could more directly claim to be making an impact on local, state, and national economies. Now, policy makers are having serious discussions about the changing role of community colleges and how they should be better used to meet the needs of a growing "Nation of Learners" (Business–Higher Education Forum, 2003). However, the community college movement suffers from sundry funding models, most of which still favor for-credit, traditional higher education programs. Even so, at least twenty-two states support discrete and motivating funding mechanisms to better inspire the workforce development mission (Warford, 2000–01). Moreover, with the impending reauthorization of the Workforce Investment Act and possible revamping of the longstanding career-focused Perkins legislation, there are signs that these states will further support the workforce development function of community colleges. And, particularly in the case of the Perkins proposals being considered by the Department of Education, there is a specific focus on supporting college and career transitions, which fully supports both workforce education and academic excellence and blends the best of the first and second waves of the community college movement (http://www.ed.gov/offices/OVAE/CCLO). All of this policy and national dialogue notwithstanding, there is still a substantial distance to go in truly helping business and industry leverage the potential of community colleges in workforce development. In short, many small and large businesses are still unaware that the community college next door can meet their training needs.

The further work that needs to be done in both internal and external connections has driven leaders to explore *best-practice models* in engaging entrepreneurial expansion (Grub, 1997; McCabe, 1997; Roueche, Taber, and Roueche, 1995). We note that this once-shunned set of trends is now so prevalent and accepted that the League for Innovation discontinued a discrete conference on workforce development in 1998, weaving the theme instead into its new Innovations conference (http://www.league.org/i2004/index.html), which explores innovations across the community college movement. Recent keynote speakers at the Innovations conference ranged from Kay McClenney, the then senior vice president of Education Commission on the States; to Tina Sung, president of the American Society for Training and Development; to Hillary Pennington, president of Jobs for the Future; to Senator Ted Kennedy; to Kweisi Mfume (2003), president of the National Association for the Advancement of Colored People. Each has spoken passionately about the need for community colleges to take on the internal and external challenges necessary and embrace the best practices possible to meet the workforce needs of their local community and the nation at large.

The notion of *fundraising* in this context is broader, including a host of entrepreneurial activities to further support the college, diversify the revenue streams, and increase the visibility of the institution. When college CEOs and trustees talk about financing and supporting their institution, the simple divisions of hard and soft money revenue streams are no longer as simple. Our college budgets are now awash with complex partnerships, interagency agreements, and corporate alliances. It's clear that the second wave has crashed to shore, and just in time to build the swell for the next. Indeed, the greater visibility and flexibility developed through entrepreneurial expansion has positioned community and technical colleges well for what is coming.

Institutional Advancement and the Third Wave

By exploring the first and second waves, we are better able to contextualize the third wave that appears poised to sweep through our movement. It is important to note that, unlike Toffler's waves, these waves are not so transformational as to supplant or suppress past transformations. Rather, these waves seem to be additive, almost synergistic. Without the comprehensive integration work of the first wave, community colleges would have been hard pressed to step up to the challenge of entrepreneurial expansion. And without the greater notoriety and increased economic and social role of the community college brought about through the second wave, we would be much less likely to truly embrace the wave that seems to be upon us: institutional advancement.

In a recent article (Milliron and de los Santos, forthcoming), we describe the results of the most recent of the national trend surveys that the League for Innovation conducts every three years. The previous two surveys, conducted in 1997 and 2000, respectively (Milliron and Leach, 1997; Milliron and Miles, 2000), were each dominated in a sense by second-wave issues, particularly workforce development–driven partnership programs and technology transitions. In the 2003 survey, there was a marked shift, with the hottest emerging trend for CEOs being the rising prominence of private fundraising. And this was not just fundraising in the first- or second-wave, hard- and soft-money business-expansion sense. This was about developing giving campaigns, capital programs, donor solicitation, and scholarship endowments. This was institutional advancement and fundraising in the broadest sense. While a number of institutions have been involved in these efforts before, now the pitch and purposes seem to have shifted. Bill Wenrich and Betheny Reid make this point quite well in Chapter Three of this volume, "It's Not the Race I Signed Up For, But It's the Race I'm In: The Role of Community College Presidents." Most seasoned community college CEOs in our survey noted the increased time expectations and trustee pressures surrounding private fundraising. Moreover, most boards searching for new presidents are clearly looking for candidates with exposure to and an interest in the art of friend- and fund-raising (Zeiss and Paneitz, 2003).

This shift is being driven by the twin forces of shrinking external fund-ing streams and the realization that community colleges are truly worthy agencies clearly behind in the fundraising game, as discussed by David Bass in Chapter Two. But, as Brenda Babitz points out so well in Chapter One, the time is upon us to step to the plate and leverage private fundraising. It is our time to truly advance our institutions by taking the next step in strengthening the connection with our constituents.

As this next wave hits, we must step forward as masters of our own des-tiny: one president in our 2003 trend survey noted that we will soon need to call ourselves publicly assisted colleges instead of publicly supported colleges because of our shrinking fixed allocations from state and local sources. This may be the final arrival of our institutions as we stand up and note our value to the extent that we are willing to ask for equal or superior private support for our vital activities. Surely our strategies and messages will be distinct, as is discussed throughout this volume; however, our arrival and transformation because of this third wave will lead to a markedly different set of internal and external issues. In particular, it will lead to the direct quest for best-practice models that work in the community college context.

There is little need to detail the clear and vital *internal* issues necessary to address as our colleges move into this next phase. The authors in this vol-ume have cogently outlined the need for faculty, staff, presidential, institu-tional board, foundation staff, and foundation board involvement and alignment. Moreover, as Tony Zeiss (Chapter Seven) and then Neil Herbkersman and Karla Hibbert-Jones (Chapter Eight) note, the move toward private fundraising must be aligned with and leverage ongoing business and industry activities along with more traditional grant-writing activities.

In addition to the internal issues explored, the authors here have well outlined the essential external connections necessary to make fundraising work. From engaging and leveraging alumni, to reaching out to business and community partners, to building one-on-one personal relationships with individuals willing to support the vital mission of our colleges, we must tell our story out loud.

Yet what has been most compelling for us has been the wide array of emerging *best practices* in fundraising. True, compared with our four-year counterparts, community colleges are relatively new to the high-stakes fundraising game. Still, what is clear from the preceding chapters is that there are, in place, solid models from which we can learn. Even as Bass and others note the clear distinction between our messages, there is ample evi-dence that we can be and are successful at "making the ask."

Riding the Third Wave

Community colleges are youngsters in higher education, barely a hundred years old, if you're willing to count the parents of the comprehensive com-munity college in the mix. Yet in this relatively short time, they have burst onto the national and international scene as key players in the educational, economic, and social milieu. Even as our society embraces the third wave outlined by Toffler as the rise of the information age, our institutions are responding well and dynamically in meeting the needs of this nation of learners.

However, if we are to reach our full potential in the midst of this societal transformation, we contend that it is imperative for us to ride the community college movement's third wave. We must embrace our worth and make the case for greater support. We well know that it is a savage inequality that although community colleges educate almost half of those in higher education—with strong majorities of ethnic minorities and women—our combined endowments do not equal even one percent of the value of four-year–sector endowments. It is now up to us to welcome institutional advancement along with the other waves and to bring our institutions to new levels of support. Indeed, we must climb atop the exciting confluence of all three waves—comprehensive integration, entrepreneurial expansion, and institutional advancement—and ride. With these forces behind the flow, we just may be able to bring the much-needed currents of learning, earning, and opportunity to *all* students.

References

Bailey, T. "The Evolving Community College: The Multiple Mission Debate." In N. Thomas (ed.), *Perspectives on the Community College,* pp. 47–49. Phoenix, Ariz.: League for Innovation in the Community College and Macomb Community College Institute for Future Studies, 2002.

Baker, G., III, and others. *Team Building for Quality: Transitions in the American Community College.* Washington, D.C.: Community College Press, 1995.

Barr, R., and Tagg, J. "From Teaching to Learning: A New Paradigm for Undergraduate Education." *Change,* 1995, 27(6), 13–25.

Bober, G. "Faculty Externships: Catalysts for TQM." *Leadership Abstracts,* 1991, 4(14). [http://www.league.org/publication/abstracts/leadership/labs1191.html]. Accessed Oct. 8, 2003.

Boggs, G. "The Learning Paradigm." *Community College Journal,* 1996, 66(3), 24–27.

Boggs, G., and Bragg, S. "Teaching the Teachers: Meeting the National Teacher Preparation Challenge." *Leadership Abstracts,* 1999, 12(1). [http://www.league.org/publication/abstracts/leadership/labs0299.htm]. Accessed Oct. 8, 2003.

Business–Higher Education Forum. "Building a Nation of Learners: The Need for Change in Teaching and Learning to Meet Global Challenges." Washington, D.C.: Business–Higher Education Forum, 2003. [http://www.acenet.edu/programs/bhef/bhef_publications.cfm?pubID=285]. Accessed Oct. 8, 2003.

Christensen, C. *The Innovator's Dilemma.* Cambridge, Mass.: Harvard Business School Press, 1997.

College Board. "Six Benefits of Community Colleges: It Might Be the Right Path for You."[http://www.collegeboard.com/article/1,,4–21–0-8169,00.html]. Accessed Oct. 8, 2003.

Davis, B., and Wessel, D. *Prosperity: The Coming 20-Year Boom and What It Means to You.* New York: Random House, 1998.

Education Commission of the States. "Community College Role in Teacher Preparation." 2002. [http://www.communitycollegepolicy.org/html/top.asp?page=/html/policy_issues_main.asp]. Accessed Oct. 8, 2003.

Gates, B. "Conversations on Community Colleges, Technology, and Tomorrow." Keynote address presented at the annual League for Innovation in the Community College Conference on Information Technology, Miami, 1998.

Greenspan, A. "Committee on Education and the Workforce Testimony." Presented at the U.S. House of Representatives, Washington, D.C., Sept. 2000.

Grub, W. *Workforce, Economic, and Community Development.* Mission Viejo, Calif.: League for Innovation in the Community College, National Center for Research in Vocational Education, National Council on Occupational Education, 1997.

Jacobs, J. "Vocational and General Education: New Relationships or Shotgun Marriage?" *Leadership Abstracts,* 1993, 6(9). [http://www.league.org/publication/abstracts/leadership/labs0993.html]. Accessed Oct. 8, 2003.

Kintzer, F. "Community Colleges Go International: Short-Cycle Education Around the World." *Leadership Abstracts,* 1998, 11(6). [http://www.league.org/publication/abstracts/leadership/labs0698.html]. Accessed Oct. 8, 2003.

McCabe, R. *The American Community College: Nexus for Workforce Development.* Mission Viejo, Calif.: League for Innovation in the Community College, 1997.

Mfume, K. "Self-Advocacy in an Uncertain Age." Keynote address presented at the Innovations conference of the League for Innovation in the Community College, Phoenix, Ariz., Mar. 2003. [http://www.league.org/publication/abstracts/ leadership/labs0403.html]. Accessed Oct. 8, 2003.

Milliron, M. "Touching Students in the Digital Age: The Move Toward Learner Relationship Management." *Learning Abstracts,* 2001, 4(1). [http://www.league.org/publication/abstracts/learning/lelabs0101.html].

Milliron, M., and de los Santos, G. "Making the Most of Community Colleges on the Road Ahead." *Community College Journal of Research and Practice, 28*(2), forthcoming.

Milliron, M., and Johnson, S. "Avoiding the Dialectic Dialogue of Dogmatic Diatribes." *Converge Magazine,* Jun.-Jul. 2002.

Milliron, M., and Leach, E. "Community Colleges Winning Through Innovation: Taking on the Changes and Choices of Leadership in the Twenty-First Century." *Leadership Abstracts,* Special Edition, 1997. [http://www.league.org/publication/abstracts/leadership/leadabccwi.html]. Accessed Oct. 8, 2003.

Milliron, M., and Miles, C. "Seven Signs on the Road Ahead for Community Colleges." In M. Milliron and C. Miles (eds.), *Taking a Big Picture Look @ Technology, Learning, and the Community College,* pp. 1–52. Mission Viejo, Calif.: League for Innovation in the Community College, 2000.

National Association of Community College Teacher Education Programs. "NACCTEP Report." Proposal presented at the inaugural Blazing the Trail conference, Phoenix, Ariz., Mar. 14–16, 2002.

Nielsen, N., Baird, D., Browning, B., and Milliron, M. (eds.). *Building a Workforce System Through Partnering.* Phoenix, Ariz.: League for Innovation in the Community College, 2003.

O'Banion, T. "A Renaissance of Innovation." Report of the Executive Director, League for Innovation in the Community College. Presented at Laguna Hills, Calif., May 1985.

O'Banion, T. "Celebrating Two Decades of Innovation." *Community, Technical, and Junior College Journal,* 1988, 58(4), 44–46.

O'Banion, T. *A Learning College for the 21st Century.* Phoenix, Ariz.: ACE/Oryx Press, 1997.

O'Banion, T., and Milliron, M. "College Conversations on Learning." *Learning Abstracts,* 2001, 4(5). [http://www.league.org/publication/abstracts/learning/lelabs0109.html]. Accessed Oct. 8, 2003.

Perez, S., and Copenhaver, C. "Certificates on Center Stage: Occupational Education for a Working Economy." *Leadership Abstracts,* 1998, 11(3). [http://www.league.org/publication/abstracts/leadership/labs0398.html]. Accessed Oct. 8, 2003.

Roueche, J., and Schultz, R. "All That Glitters Is Not Gold." *Journal of Higher Education*, Feb. 1966, 37(2), 91–93.

Roueche, J., Taber, L., and Roueche, S. *The Company We Keep: Collaboration in the Community College*. Washington, D.C.: Community College Press, 1995.

Spanbauer, S. "Quality: A Business Prescription for Community and Technical Colleges." *Leadership Abstracts*, 1992, 5(3). [http://www.league.org/publication/abstracts/leadership/labs0392.html]. Accessed Oct. 8, 2003.

Tapscott, D. *The Digital Economy: Promise and Peril in the Age of Networked Intelligence*. New York: McGraw-Hill, 1998.

Tapscott, D. "The Rise of the Net Generation in Higher Education." Keynote address presented at the annual League for Innovation in the Community College Conference on Information Technology, Anaheim, Calif., Nov. 16, 2000.

Toffler, A. *The Third Wave*. New York: Bantam, 1989.

Warford, L. "Redesigning the System to Meet the Workforce Training Needs of the Nation." *Leadership Abstracts*, 1995, 8(1). [http://www.league.org/publication/abstracts/leadership/labs0195.html]. Accessed Oct. 8, 2003.

Warford, L. "Funding Lifelong Learning: A National Priority." *Community College Journal*, Dec. 2000/Jan. 2001.

Wilson, C. "The Community College as a Learning-Centered Organization." In N. Thomas, A. Lorenzo, and M. Milliron (eds.), *Perspectives on the Community College: A Journey of Discovery*, pp. 23–26. Phoenix, Ariz.: League for Innovation in the Community College, Macomb Community College Institute for Future Studies, 2002.

Zeiss, T., and Paneitz, B. "Weathering the Storm: Positive Reactions to Negative Budgets." *Leadership Abstracts*, 2003, 16(6). [http://www.league.org/publication/abstracts/leadership/labs0603.html]. Accessed Oct. 8, 2003.

Zook, G. *Higher Education for American Democracy: A Report to the President's Commission on Higher Education*. New York: Harper and Brothers, 1947.

MARK DAVID MILLIRON *is president and CEO of the League for Innovation in the Community College.*

GERARDO E. DE LOS SANTOS *is vice president and COO of the League for Innovation in the Community College.*

BOO BROWNING *is associate editor at the League for Innovation in the Community College.*

11

This chapter summarizes resources from the literature on development and fundraising.

Sources and Information: Development and Fundraising Within Community Colleges

Edward Francis Ryan

Faced with significant budget constraints, state governments and local municipalities have been reducing the financial support they provide to public colleges and universities. To deal with these funding shortfalls, community colleges have begun searching for alternate sources of funding. Rather than raise tuition, which would limit access for many students, these colleges have instead increased their fundraising activities by creating development offices, establishing foundations, and embarking on capital campaigns. While efforts are beginning to take hold on a number of campuses, the research related to fundraising and development is still growing. The first pieces to emerge, developed in large part by successful practitioners, provide strategies that institutions could employ when creating development programs. More recently, scholars have conducted a number of studies that survey those responsible for fundraising on their campuses. A majority of these pieces discuss the challenges development offices face, practices that are most successful, and issues emerging within the field.

This chapter summarizes resources from the literature on various types of fundraising and development activities, the role institutional actors have in the fundraising and development process, and the best practices that have emerged. Educational Resource Information Center (ERIC) documents, those followed by an "ED" number, may be read on microfiche at approximately nine hundred libraries throughout the world. Most documents may be ordered on microfiche or in paper copy from the ERIC Document Reproduction Service at 800–443-ERIC. For a list of libraries

New Directions for Community Colleges, no. 124, Winter 2003   © Wiley Periodicals, Inc.

housing ERIC microfiche documents, contact the ERIC Clearinghouse for Community Colleges at 800–832–8256 or via e-mail at ericcc@ucla.edu. Journal articles may be acquired through libraries, from the journal publisher, or for a fee from the article reproduction vendor, Ingenta (e-mail help@ingenta.com; phone 617–395–4046; toll-free 800–296–2221; or Web site http://www.ingenta.com).

Types of Development Activities

As fundraising and development activities within the community colleges are a relatively recent occurrence, those within the field are still in the process of identifying and differentiating key concepts. This section defines the notion of development and identifies the different types of activities currently being employed.

Worth, M. J. (ed.). *Educational Fund Raising: Principles and Practices.* Phoenix, Ariz.: Oryx Press, 1993.

Worth opens this edited volume by defining the term *development* and situating it within the broader context of the institution. For Worth, development consists of "all the programs and activities by which the college or university seeks gifts and grants from private sources to support its program and to build long-term strength through improvements to its facilities and additions to its endowments" (p. 5). While Worth notes that the term often is used interchangeably with *fundraising,* development connotes a more sophisticated process of planning in which officers create a list of specific institutional needs, conduct research to find a pool of potential donors, and match the needs of the institution with the interests of the donors. "Only when these initial steps in the development process have been achieved is the institution ready for fund raising, which in its narrowest sense means solicitation or simply asking for gifts" (p. 7).

After defining the development, Worth argues that, within the broader institutional context, development offices along with alumni relations, enrollment management, external communications, governmental relations, and public relations fall under the purview of institutional advancement. This function encompasses "all activities and programs undertaken by an institution to develop understanding and support from all its constituencies in order to achieve it goals in securing such resources as students, faculty, and dollars" (p. 5). While all of these offices work in collaboration to advance the mission of the university, each has its own focus.

Remaining chapters provide the reader with descriptions of the many different types of development efforts. They discuss in detail donor characteristics; annual giving, major gifts, and planned giving programs; capital campaigns; and corporate fundraising. Together, the chapters provide both a broad overview of the field and specific strategies to employ when fundraising.

Bauer, D. G. *Administering Grants, Contracts and Funds: Evaluating and Improving Your Grants System.* New York: Collier Macmillan, 1989.

Bauer, a professional grant consultant, provides his readers with a detailed process of how to obtain and administer grants. Bauer begins by noting that too many grant administrators judge success based on the number and dollar amount of grants received. And while these may be easy measures to gauge, they do not necessarily help the organization judge whether the grant-writing activities are being used to effectively promote institutional goals. Bauer contends that grant administrators must first determine what the organization's key goals are and then base their evaluation on the grant office's ability to obtain funds that support those goals. Bauer concludes by discussing several strategies institutions can employ to strengthen their applications. Specifically, he suggests that applicants examine the proposals of organizations that have successfully applied for funding from a particular agency in order to better understand the expectations of the granting agency.

The Role of Institutional Actors

Much of the literature suggests that a number of institutional actors significantly affect the success of development and fundraising efforts, including the college president, the chief development officer, the institutional board of directors, the foundation board of directors, and alumni. This section provides examples of research examining the roles the various actors play in fundraising activities.

College Presidents

Cook, W. B. "Fundraising and the College Presidency in an Era of Uncertainty." *Journal of Higher Education,* 1997, 68(1), 53–86.

In this review of the literature, the author uses a historical lens to explain how public funding for higher education has dwindled over the past twenty years, causing colleges and universities to bolster their fundraising efforts. Cook suggests this change has impacted the office of the presidency in that fundraising experience has become a requisite for those interested in presidential positions. As one source noted, "when governing boards go hunting for presidents, it's often the candidate's fundraising rather than academic talents that catch the eye" (p. 74). Cook also notes that fundraising has become an important measure of presidential success. Citing a number of former presidents and two research studies, Cook argues that past presidents are remembered more for their ability to fundraise than for their ability to improve the quality of the institution.

Cook then discusses the role presidents play in fundraising efforts, using a football analogy to liken the president to a quarterback for being the institutional leader that orchestrates the process. In this role, the president needs to focus his or her efforts on providing administrative leadership in such areas as developing strategy, selecting and supervising key development officers, engaging the board of trustees in the process, recruiting campaign volunteers, and articulating the campaign vision. Cook concludes the piece by discussing some of the challenges presidents face, noting that fundraising can absorb an enormous amount of the president's time and cause stress in his or her life.

Glass, Jr., J. C., and Jackson, K. L. "A New Role for Community College Presidents: Private Fund Raiser and Development Team Leader." *Community College Journal of Research and Practice,* 1998, 22, 575–590.

Aware that more than half of all newly appointed community college presidents lack any significant fundraising experience, Glass and Jackson provide a detailed explanation of the tasks presidents must fulfill in order to be successful. Borrowing from the work of Smith (1986) and Vaughn (1989), the authors argue that presidents should develop and articulate an institutional mission, create a climate of support from other institutional actors, serve as an example by personally giving, and plan fundraising strategies. They then identify other institutional actors who are involved in fundraising efforts. As trustees of community colleges usually are either publicly elected or appointed officials, they may not have the skills nor connections needed to be successful fundraisers. The authors suggest that trustees who lack fundraising skills should thus play a more supportive role, helping to develop and endorse the college foundation. Glass and Jackson then describe the roles foundation directors and resource development officers play and conclude with a discussion of how training can help the different players work together more effectively.

Chief Development Officer

Worth, M. J., and Asp II, J. A. *The Development Officer in Higher Education: Toward an Understanding of the Role.* ASHE-ERIC Higher Education Report, no 4. Washington, D.C.: George Washington University, Graduate School of Education and Human Development, 1994. (ED 382107)

Although the position of Chief Development Officer (CDO) is becoming more common on college and university campuses, few researchers have defined the roles these officers play or described the ways they interact with other institutional leaders. Worth and Asp fill this void, providing the reader with a conceptual overview of the position. Based on a review of the literature, the authors name four roles that development officers can play: fundraiser, catalyst, manager, and leader. And while it can be debated whether a CDO should dedicate him- or herself to any one of these roles, Worth and Asp suggest that most probably assume more than one at any given time.

Fundraisers are seen as solicitors of gifts who first form strong relationships with potential donors and then inspire them to give. In this role, the CDO pays less attention to donor research and managerial issues and more to the development of strong bonds with donors and alumni. This role is markedly different from that of the catalyst, who organizes development activities but does not play a role in solicitation. Catalysts coordinate and facilitate the development process by "continually reminding, prompting and urging trustees, the president, faculty, and staff of their responsibilities in the major gift area" (p. 20). In some ways, catalysts and managers are similar in that they are removed from the solicitation process. However, managers concentrate more on the internal workings of the fundraising machine, ensuring that all components are functioning. Specifically, they attend to special-event planning, donor research, publication development, and resource management. Finally, the role of the leader is probably most distinct in that he or she focuses less on the specifics of development and plays a larger role in long-term institutional planning. Worth and Asp conclude by addressing several practical questions that deal with the relationship between the CDO and the institution's president and trustees and the CDO's role with institutional planning and gift solicitation.

Institutional Board of Directors

McDonald, J. G. *Changing State Policies to Strengthen Public University and College Trustee Selection and Education.* (AGB Public Policy Paper Series, no. 95–2). Washington, D.C.: Association of Governing Boards of Universities and Colleges, 1995. (ED 412829)

Concerned that many individuals elected or appointed to the boards of directors of public institutions may not have the skills, abilities, or requisite knowledge needed to effectively carry out their roles as board members and fundraisers, the Association of Governing Boards (AGB) of Universities and Colleges has drafted a number of position papers on the selection and training of regents and trustees. In this AGB paper, McDonald reports on the efforts of four states that have revised their selection process and implemented orientation programs. She describes the efforts of Kentucky, Massachusetts, Minnesota, and Oklahoma and provides readers with an analysis based on in-depth interviews of those who participated in the change efforts. While each state took a somewhat different approach, they all essentially shifted from a process in which the governor appointed political allies to one in which a bipartisan committee screened qualified applicants and provided the governor with a list of recommended choices.

Through her interviews, McDonald found that the new selection process was seen as an improvement over its predecessor, as it created a standard set of criteria against which all candidates were evaluated. It fostered a more democratic process by allowing those who had previously been excluded for lack of political connections to participate. However, participants noted that the revised screening process was time consuming and became burdensome for those on the screening committee. McDonald concludes the piece by discussing the perceptions of those who participated in the trustee orientation and training programs. While a number of the issues raised are system specific, McDonald provides general advice to states considering such programs and suggests that program planners should be inclusive and seek input from all constituencies within the state's higher education community.

Foundation Board of Directors

Simic, C. R. *The Role of the Foundation Board.* Washington, D.C.: Association of Governing Boards of Universities and Colleges, 1998. (ED 428596)

In 1998, the American Association of Community Colleges (AACC) found that nearly all of the 631 institutions that responded to its survey on community college foundations have or are in the process of developing a foundation to support their fundraising efforts. Such foundations have become increasingly popular among institutional leaders as they provide public colleges and universities a certain amount of fiscal flexibility not enjoyed by other state-sponsored organizations. Aware of the increased role these organizations play, the AGB has developed a number of resources to help institutions build strong foundations. In this AGB paper, Simic provides an overview of how foundations can be used most effectively. The author raises several issues most foundation board members encounter and provides strategies to meet these issues head on. Specifically, he discusses board-member recruitment, gift solicitation, relationship building between governing and foundation boards, and goal setting.

Alumni

Nazzaro, J. P. *Community College Alumni: Partners in Resource Development.* Paper presented at the Junior and Community College Institute's Alumni Development Workshop, Washington, D.C., Aug. 1992. (ED 358904)

A common theme in the literature is that community college alumni often have weak ties to their institutions, making it difficult to solicit gifts from them. Nazzaro chronicles the success of one college in developing an alumni giving program. In this single-institution case study, the author shows how County College in Morris, New Jersey, developed an effective alumni program designed to "create pride among current students, develop a prelude to funding efforts, develop long term commitments, and develop alumni networks as entrees to corporations" (p. 4).

To achieve these goals, the institution created a marketing campaign, which showcased five alumni who had become leaders in the local community. These alumni became spokespeople for the campus, helped kick off an alumni fundraising drive, and served as a conduit to the local business community. The community college also worked with a publishing company to create an alumni directory—used by alumni to locate classmates and by the college as a research tool to find corporations with large concentrations of County College alumni. County College then established alumni chapters at these corporations and began soliciting funds from them.

Best Practices

A number of research studies have examined institutional and systemwide efforts to create and strengthen development activities. In many of these studies, the authors discuss the practices that have been most successful and the issues still confronting fundraisers. This section describes the best practices and identifies emerging issues.

Haire, C. M., and Dodson-Pennington, L. S. "Taking the Road Less Traveled: A Journey in Collaborative Resource Development." *Community College Journal of Research and Practice,* 2002, 26, 61–75.

In this single-institution case study, the authors chronicle the successful efforts by Southwestern Community College (North Carolina) to obtain $15 million in external grants by forging collaborative partnerships with other local colleges, community-based organizations, and a regional university. In their analysis, Haire and Dodson-Pennington argue that the success of the partnership can be attributed to four key elements: a college culture that supports and values broad-based collaboration; long-standing, meaningful partnerships; solid resource-development strategies; and well-cultivated, creative project ideas. After describing how each of these elements played a key role in the success of their fundraising efforts, the authors describe the collaborative projects in depth.

Community Link: Because the campus is located in a sparsely populated region of the country, college administrators developed Community Link, an interactive, instructional television network that provides students who live far from the college the opportunity to attend classes without traveling to the campus. Although an expensive endeavor, the college was able to forge links with a local telephone carrier and the North Carolina Public Utilities Commission to obtain federal funding for the project.

Collegiate Connections: This program works with middle and high school students to improve academic readiness, bolster student persistence in high school, and increase college enrollment. As part of the initiative, students who commit to staying in school and who volunteer in the community can receive a grant that pays for two years of tuition at Southwestern Community College. To fund this program, institutional administrators have worked with over five hundred businesses, civic groups, and individuals to raise $450,000. The fundraising efforts have been successful in part because the donations are seen as an investment in the economic future of the region.

Appalachian Access: Community college administrators found that the cost of bringing internet service to the region is extremely high. However, aware that information and connectivity will play an increasing important role in the future economic success of the community, community leaders and college administrators have begun working with the telecommunications industry to bring affordable Internet services to the region. While this initiative is still in its infancy, the college is working with local vendors to help fund this program.

Smokey Mountain Knowledge Network: This effort creates mechanisms that allow multiple organizations to purchase specialized computer applications as a group and use them at each of their organizations. By this system of sharing, the college and its partners are able to pay less for new technology and share costs associated with training and development.

Barber, J. *State University of New York and City University of New York Staff Study: Private Fundraising at SUNY and CUNY.* (Report 96-D-1). Albany: New York State Office of the Comptroller, 1998. (ED 418753)

Between 1996 and 1998, research analysts from the New York State Office of the Comptroller were asked by administrators at the State University of New York (SUNY) and the City University of New York (CUNY) to conduct an assessment of both systems' fundraising efforts. Using data from the Council for Aid to Education, Barber compared the fundraising efforts of the two New York systems to those of the top twenty fundraising institutions—a sample of institutions with similar academic programs that employ comparable development practices. In his analysis, Barber found that both systems raised significantly fewer funds than the top fundraisers despite being two of the largest systems of higher education in the country. Additionally, SUNY institutions were less successful in their fundraising as compared to both their development and academic peers, whereas some CUNY institutions were more successful than some of their development peers but trailed their academic peers.

After identifying that both systems were limited in their fundraising capabilities, the researcher suggests that they consider employing new strategies to strengthen their fundraising abilities: commit staff and resources to development, recruit and employ staff with significant experience in fundraising, maintain alumni and donor records, pursue prospect research for donations and major gifts, create an annual fund, develop a planned giving program, and promote good relations with corporations and foundations. Barber concludes this piece by illustrating how other successful fundraising institutions employed these best practices to strengthen their development activities.

Roha, T. A. *State University-Related Foundation and the Issues of Independence.* (AGB Occasional Paper, no. 39). Washington, D.C.: Association of Governing Boards of Universities and Colleges, 2000. (ED 442326)

In the past few years, a number of news organizations using federal and state Freedom of Information Acts have filed lawsuits against public college and university foundations, seeking information about the foundations, their donors, and their fundraising activities. The lawsuits suggest that these foundations are not private in that they use land, facilities, and resources paid for with tax dollars. Accordingly, the complaints argue that foundations, which receive public support, are public entities and must open their records for public review. These lawsuits are of great concern for private foundations as they may affect the foundation's ability to raise and spend resources and ensure donor privacy.

Roha, who provides legal counsel to a number of colleges and universities, has written this paper to help public institutions understand the legal ramifications of recent court rulings and protect themselves from potential lawsuits. He begins by providing an overview of recent court cases, explaining the reasons behind the initial complaint, the issues involved, and the decisions made by the courts. In each case, Roha found that the courts' decisions were based on the extent to which the foundation received resources—whether financial, human, or physical—from the institution.

Roha concludes this piece with strategies for distancing the foundation from the institution and protecting its standing as a private organization. He suggests that foundations should create an independent board of directors, pay for any office space that is located on the campus or owned by the university, pay foundation employees with foundation resources, retain and pay for independent counsel, voluntarily release information requested by outside organizations, regularly release reports that chronicle the foundation's activities, and create an agreement between the foundation and the institution that clearly defines the relationship between the two organizations and affirms the foundation's independence.

Additional Sources

In additional to the aforementioned research, a number of additional works provide information and research on new issues facing fundraising and development efforts. Most of these documents can be found in online journals or through the ERIC system.

Bornstein, R. "Venture Philanthropy: A Boon to Academe?" *Trusteeship,* 2001, *9*(5), 24–27.

Carberry, G. E. "Cultivating Entrepreneurs: A Shift in Corporate Fundraising." *Community College Journal,* 2002, *72*(4), 24–27.

Glass, J. C., Jr., and Jackson, K. L. "Integrating Resource Planning and Institutional Planning." *Community College Journal of Research and Practice,* 1998, *22,* 715–739.

Glass, J. C., Jr., and Jackson, K. L. "Emerging Trends and Critical Issues Affecting Private Fundraising Among Community Colleges." *Community College Journal of Research and Practice,* 2000, *24,* 729–744.

Hedgepth, R. C. *How Public Colleges and University Foundations Pay for Fund-Raising.* Washington, D.C.: Association of Governing Boards of Universities and Colleges, 2000. (ED 446572)

Keener, B. J., Carrier, S. M., and Meaders, S. J. "Resource Development in Community Colleges." *Community College Journal of Research and Practice,* 2002, *26,* 7–23.

Phelan, J. F. (ed.). *College and University Foundations: Serving America's Public Higher Education. A Handbook for Members and Chief Executives of Foundations and Governing Boards.* Washington, D.C.: Association of Governing Boards of Universities and Colleges, 1997. (ED 406925)

Ruskin, K. B., and Achilles, C. M. *Grantwriting, Fundraising and Partnerships: Strategies That Work.* Thousand Oaks, Calif.: Corwin Press, 1995.

Smith, G.T. "The Chief Executive and Advancement." In A.W. Rowland (ed.), *Handbook of Institutional Advancement: A Modern Guide to Executive Management, Institutional Relations, Fund-raising, Alumni Administration, Government Relations, Publications, Periodicals, and Enrollment Management.* (2nd ed.) San Francisco: Jossey-Bass, 1986.

Vaughan, G. B. *Leadership in Transition: The Community College Presidency.* New York: American Council on Education and Macmillan, 1989.

Worth, M. J. *New Strategies for Educational Fund Raising.* Phoenix, Ariz.: Oryx Press, 2002.

EDWARD FRANCIS RYAN is a doctoral student in the Graduate School of Education and Information Studies at the University of California–Los Angeles.

INDEX

Administering Grants, Contracts and Funds: Evaluating and Improving Your Grants System (Bauer), 97
Administration, sustaining engaged, 36–37
Advancement model, 64
AGB. *See* Association of Governing Boards of Universities and Colleges
Alliance for Employee Growth and Development, 60
Alumni: development, 75–79; giving, 11–12; and the MCC Foundation, 75–77; role of, 100–101; steps to success in developing, 77–78
American Association of Community and Junior Colleges, 9, 57, 68, 83, 84, 100
American Society for Training and Development, 88
Annual fund, 10
Appalachian Access project, 102
Archivist role, 68
Asp, J. A., II, 98, 99
Association of Governing Boards of Universities and Colleges, 5, 17, 99, 100, 102
"Astounding Transformations" (*University Business*), 21
Australia, 84

Babitz, B., 5, 90
Bailey, T., 83
Baird, D., 87
Baker, G., III, 86
Barber, J., 102
Barr, R., 87
Bass, D., 15, 90
Bauer, D. G., 63, 67, 97
Beasley, K., 64
Bellevue Community College (Washington), 57
Benchmark Practices for Local Economies (Regional Technology Strategies, Inc.), 22, 23
Bennett, B., 19
Best practice models, 88, 101–103
Birmingham, K., 23

BISNET. *See* Business and Industry Network (BISNET)
Blockbuster International, 43
Blong, J., 19
Bober, G., 86
Boggs, G., 86, 87
BOOK Limited, 42
Bragg, S., 86, 87
Breneman, D., 16
Broward Community College (BCC; Florida), 7, 41–44; Endowed Teaching Chair Committee, 43; Foundation, 43
Browning, B., 81, 87
Brumbach, M., 68
Budget developer, role of, 67–68
Buechner, F., 30
Burlington Northern Santa Fe Railroad, 57, 86
Bush, G. W., 60
Business and Industry Network (BISNET), 85
Business partnerships, 56–57, 59–60

Cabrillo Community College (California), 7
California colleges, 17
Callan, P., 18
Canada, 84
Capital campaign, 11
Capital Community College (Hartford, Connecticut), 21–23
Carlson, C. J., 47
Carrier, S., 19
Caterpillar Corporation, 57
Cedar Rapids, Iowa, 35; Chamber of Commerce, 37
Central Piedmont Community College (CPCC; Charlotte, North Carolina), 56, 58–61; Corporate and Continuing Educational division, 61; Pathways to Employment program, 60
Change: resources for, 23–25; substantive, 21–23
Changing State Policies to Strengthen Public University and College Trustee Selection and Education (McDonald), 100

Charles Stewart Mott Community College (Flint, Michigan), 21, 23; Regional Technology Center, 21
Charlotte, North Carolina, 56, 59, 60; Chamber of Commerce, 60; and Charlotte-Douglas International Airport, 56
Cheerleader role, 68
Chief Advancement Officer (CAO), 8
Chief Development Officer, 98, 99
Christensen, C., 81
Chronicle of Higher Education, 5–6, 18
"Chronicle Survey of Public Opinion on Higher Education" (Chronicle of Higher Education), 18–19
Cisco Systems, 56–57; Network Academies, 86
City University of New York (CUNY), 102
Cleveland, Ohio, 27; Marathon, 27
College Board, 84
College President, 8
Collegiate Connections program, 101
Commitment, organizational, 63–64
Communications, 12
Community college advancement: contexts for change in, 15–25; examples of substantive change in, 21–23; and privatization, 16–17; and public purpose, 17–19; and resources for change, 23–25; state university models and community contexts in, 19–21
Community College Alumni: Partners in Resource Development (Nazzaro), 100–101
Community College Business and Industry Alliance, 85, 86
Community college foundation: and fundraising process, 7–8; and institution wide responsibility, 8–10; and quest for private support, 6–7; and specific strategies to build support, 10–13; strategies for leveraging, 6–7
Community College Journal, 6
Community College Journal of Research and Practice, 98, 101–103
Community Link project, 101
Competencies, 68–70; behavior, 69–70; and customer service, 69; and effective communication strategies, 69; and high integrity, 69–70; and project-planning and management techniques, 68; technical, 68–69
Comprehensive integration, first wave and, 82–85

Consultants, 66
Cook, W. B., 97, 98
Copenhaver, C., 86
Council for Advancement and Support of Education, 12
Council for Aid to Education, 7
Council for Resource Development, 23, 68, 70
County College (Morris, New Jersey), 100–101
Critical chain (Goldratt), 65
CUNY. See City University of New York

Dallas Community College District (DCCCD), 29; Foundation, 22, 29; Rising Star program, 22, 29
Dallas-Ft. Worth Airport, 29
Davies, G., 17
Davis, B., 28, 53, 86, 87
Dayton, Ohio, 70
de los Santos, G. E., 81, 82, 89
Delta College (University City, Michigan), 7, 57
Development activities, types of, 96–97
Development Officer in Higher Education: Toward an Understanding of the Role (Worth and Asp), 99
DeVry University, 54–55
Dickens, C., 15, 16
Dodson-Pennington, L. S., 101–103
Donor stewardship, 12
Dreamer role, 67
Duke Energy Global Technical Workforce Development Initiative, 61
Dynamic Foundation for Fundraising: A Detailed Compendium for Organizing or Reorganizing for Success (Phelan), 24

Editor, 67
Education Commission on the States, 2002, 86–88
Educational enterprises, 53–55
Educational Fund Raising: Principles and Practices (Worth), 96
Educational Resource Information Center (ERIC), 95, 96; Clearinghouse for Community Colleges, 95, 96; Document Reproduction Service, 95
Entrepreneurial activities, 57–58, 60–61
Entrepreneurial expansion, second wave and, 82, 83–89
ERIC. See Educational Resource Information Center
ESL programs, 60, 61

Europe, 84
Evaluation expert role, 68
Executive leaders, 66
External partners, 66
External stakeholders, 50

Facilitator, 67
Family Dollar Stores, 59
Financial team, 66
Finisher role, 68
First wave, 82–85
Focused initiatives, 11
Ford Foundation, 59
Foundation Board, 9–10, 100
Foundation office, 64–69
Freedom Fest (Cedar Rapids, Iowa), 35
Freedom of Information Acts, 103
Friendraising, 6, 35
"Fundraising and the College Presidency in an Era of Uncertainty" (*Journal of Higher Education*), 97–98
Fundraising objectives, based on institutional priorities, 65

Gates, B., 86
General Accounting Office, 59
General Motors Corporation (GM), 57
G.I. Bill, 83
Gitomer, J., 69
Glass, J., 19, 20, 23, 98
GM-Delta Automotive Service Educational Program, 57
Goldratt, E., 65, 66; Theory of Constraints, 65
Grants Development Office, 63; and clearly defined roles, 64–65; competencies required within, 68–70; and Compression Planning with Storyboarding, 69; documented processes of, 65–66; and example of joint public and private development, 70–72; and fundraising objectives based on institutional priorities, 65; and organizational commitment, 63–64; professional development for personnel of, 70; role of key players within, 66; roles of, 67–68; and strategic organizational structures, 64–69
Greenspan, A., 86
Grub, W., 88

Hagerstown Community College (Maryland), 22
Haire, C. M., 101–103
Hall, M. R., 24

Hartford, Connecticut, 22
Havens, J., 6
Hebel, S., 18, 19
Hedgepeth, R., 12
Herbkersman, N., 63, 90
Hibbert-Jones, K., 63, 90
Hibbing Community College (Minnesota), 22
Higher Education Act (1965), 83
Higher Education for an American Democracy (Zook), 82
Hinterthuer, R., 22
Hooks, W., 23
Humber Institute of Technology and Advanced Learning (Toronto), 55, 56

IBM, 85
Illinois Central Community College, 57
Image, enhancing, 34–35
Information technology curriculum, 57
Ingenta (article reproduction vendor), 96
Innovation, 37–39
Institution actors, role of, 97–101
Institutional advancement, and third wave, 82, 89–90
Institutional board of directors, 99, 100
Institutional image, 12
Internal stakeholders, 50–51
Internet, 81
ITT Educational Services, 54–55

Jackson, K., 19, 20, 23, 98
Jacobs, J., 83
Jarvis, R., 19
Jobs for the Future study (Ford Foundation), 59, 88
Johnson, B. L., 83
Johnson County Community College (JCCC; Overland Park, Kansas), 57, 85, 86; Center for Business and Technology (CBT), 56; Child Development Center, 48–49; connecting mission of, with student needs, 48–49; Dollars for Scholars Auction, 50; and engaging supporters in meaningful activities, 49–51; and Johnson Countian of the Year, 49; and weaving foundation into culture of college, 47–51
Johnson, R. A., 6
Johnson, S., 87
Joliet Junior College, 82–85

Kansas City, Missouri, 85
Kansas City Regional Council for Higher Education, 85

Kaplan, A. E., 7, 15
Katsinas, S., 28
Keener, B. J., 7, 9, 12, 19
Kelley, S., 23
Kennedy, E., 88
Kentucky, 99; Community and Technical College System, 84
Kerzner, H., 68, 69
Kintzer, F., 84
Kirkwood Community College (Cedar Rapids, Iowa): Board of Trustees, 33–39; Facilities Foundation, 35; Jazz under the Stars, 35; Kirkwood Foundation, 35; Resource Development Department, 36
Kodak, 85

Lane Community College (Eugene, Oregon), 58
Leach, E., 89
League for Innovation in the Community College, 57, 83–85, 88, 89
Louisiana Technical and Community College System, 84
Lovett, C., 16

Machanic, K., 12
Malaysia, 55
Management, 13
Maricopa Community College (Phoenix, Arizona), 60, 86
Marketing, 12
Massachusetts, 99
McCabe, R., 88
McClenney, K., 88
McDonald, J. G., 99, 100
McNellis, J., 69
Meaders, S., 19
Mfume, K., 88
MGT, Inc., 59
Miami University (Middletown, Ohio), Applied Research Center, 70, 71
Miami-Dade College, 21, 23
Microsoft Corporation, 56–57, 60; IT Academies, 86
Miles, C., 86, 89
Milliron, M. D., 81, 82, 86, 87, 89
Minnesota, 99
Mitvalsky, C. W., 33
Monroe Community College (MCC; Rochester, New York), 7, 75–78; Alumni Hall of Fame, 76; Creating a Legacy campaign, 76; Foundation, 10, 11, 75–77; Gold Star Gala, 76; Holocaust Genocide Studies Project, 11;

Salute to Excellence, 76; Scholarship Open, 76
Montgomery Community College (Maryland), 7
Montgomery County (Ohio), 70, 71
Motorola University, 86
Mott Community College. See Charles Stewart Mott Community College

"Nation of Learners" (Business-Higher Education Forum), 87
National Alliance of Business, 59
National Alliance of Community College Teacher Education Programs, 60
National Association for the Advancement of Colored People (NAACP), 88
National Association of College and University Officers, 15
National Association of Community College Teacher Education Programs, 86, 87
National Association of State Budget Officers, 17
National Center for Public Policy and Higher Education, 18
National Science Foundation, 57
Nazzaro, J. P., 100–101
"New Role for Community College Presidents: Private Fund Raiser and Development Team Leader" (Community College Journal of Research and Practice), 98
New Strategies for Fundraising (Worth), 19
New York State: Council for Aid to Education, 102; Office of the Comptroller, 102
Newcomen Society of the United States, 59
Newton, W., 33
Nielsen, N., 33, 87
Ningbo University (China), 56
North Arkansas College, 22
North Arkansas Partnership for Health Education (NAPHE), 22
North Arkansas Regional Medical Center, 22
North Carolina: Department of Social Services, 60; Public Utilities Commission, 101; State Employment and Security Commission, 60
Norwalk Community College (Connecticut), 7
Novak, R., 17

O'Banion, T., 83, 87
Ohio legislature, 71
Oklahoma, 99
Olson, J., 22
Oregon University System, 19
Organizational commitment, 63–64
Organizational structure, 64–69

Padron, E., 21
Paneitz, B., 89, 90
Penn State University, 55
Pennington, H., 88
Perez, S., 86
Perkins legislation, 87
Phelan, J., 25
Pierce, D., 9
Planned gifts, 11
Planner role, 67
Potter, W., 17
Pounce theory, 30
Presidents, community college: and Broward Community College Experience, 41–44; fundraising roles of, 29–31; and need for new funding opportunities, 28–29; role of, 27–28, 97–98; and support of college's foundation, 41–46
"Private Support for Our Public University" (University of Maine Foundation), 24
Private support, quest for, 6–7
Privatization, 16–17
Project champion, 66
Public purpose, 17–19

Realist role, 67
Regional Technology Strategies, Inc., 22, 23
Reid, B. L., 22, 27, 89
Research model, 64
Researcher role, 67
Resource development, 12
Revenue: and business partnerships, 56–57; and contracted services, 55–56; and educational enterprises, 53–55; and enterprising college model, 58–61; and entrepreneurial activities, 57–58; generating new sources of, 53–61
Roha, T., 35, 102, 103
Role of the Foundation Board (Simic), 100
Roles, clearly defined, and foundation office, 64–69
Roueche, J. E., 6, 83, 88

Roueche, S. D., 6, 88
Rowland, J., 22
Rubenzahl, I., 22
Ryan, E. F., 95
Ryan, G. J., 12

San Diego Community College District: Corporate Council, 57
Sanford, Florida, 44
Santa Barbara Community College (California), 7
Sausner, R., 21, 22
Schervish, P., 6
Schriver, K., 67
Schultz, R., 83
Seattle Community College, 58
Second wave, 83–89
Selingo, J., 18
Seminole Community College (SCC; Florida), 41–46; Dream Auction, 44, 45; President's Club, 45
Services, 12; contracted, 55–56, 59
Sevier, R., 23
Shaink, R., 21
Simic, C. R., 100
Sinclair Community College (Dayton, Ohio), 63, 64, 70; Board of Trustees, 65, 70; Community College Foundation, 65; Fast Forward Center, 70, 71; Foundation, 71
Sinclair Community College (Dayton, Ohio) Grants Development Office, 63; and clearly defined roles, 64–65; competencies required within, 68–70; and Compression Planning with Storyboarding, 69; documented processes of, 65–66; and example of joint public and private development, 70–72; and fundraising objectives based on institutional priorities, 65; and organizational commitment, 63–64; professional development for personnel of, 70; roles of, 67–68; and strategic organizational structures, 64–69
Smith, N. J., 12, 98
Smokey Mountain Knowledge Network, 102
Southeast Asia, 84
Southeastern Community College (North Carolina), 22
Southwestern Community College (North Carolina), 101–102
Spanbauer, S., 86
Special Events, 10–11
Spencer, L., 68

Spencer, S., 68
State University of New York and City University of New York Staff Study: Private Fundraising at SUNY and CUNY (Barber), 102
State University of New York (SUNY), 7, 102
State University-Related Foundation and the Issues of Independence (Roha), 102
Strategic Planning in Higher Education (Sevier), 23
Structures, strategic organizational, 64–69
Sung, T., 88
SUNY. *See* State University of New York
Support team, 66

Taber, L., 88
Tagg, J., 87
"Taking the Road Less Traveled: A Journey in Collaborative Resource Development' (*Community College Journal of Research and Practice*), 101–103
Tapscott, D., 81, 86
Tarance, Z., 54, 55
Theory of Constraints (Goldratt), 65
Third wave, 81; institutional advancement and, 89–90; riding, 90–91
Toffler, A., 81, 84, 86, 91
Toffler, H., 81
Trans-Atlantic Technology and Training Alliance, 22
Trotter, M., 28
Truman Commission Report, 82
Trustees, community college, 8; and encouraging innovation, 37–39; and enhancing image, 34–35; and overseeing and supporting foundation, 35–36; role of, in supporting foundation, 33; and sustaining engaged administration, 36–37

Uchitelle, L., 28
United States Department of Agriculture, 22

United States Department of Education, 88
United States Department of Labor, Employment and Training Administration, 71
United Way, 43, 58
University Business, 21
University of California, Los Angeles, 78, 83
University of Maine Foundation, 24
University of North Carolina (Charlotte), 60
University of Phoenix, 54–55
University of Texas System, 16

Valencia Community College (Orlando, Florida), 23
van der Werf, M., 6
"Vocational and General Education: New Relationship or Shotgun Marriage" (*Leadership Abstracts*), 83
Voluntary Support of Education 2002 (Kaplan), 7

Warford, L., 86, 87
"We Mean Business: Policies for Partnerships in Industry and Education" (League for Innovation), 85
Wellman, J., 5
Wenrich, J. W., 22, 27, 89
Wessel, D., 28, 53, 86, 87
Wilson, C., 87
Workforce 2000 conference (League for Innovation), 86
Workforce Investment Act, 87
Workforce Investment Act Board (North Carolina), 60
Worth, M. J., 7, 19, 96, 98, 99
Writer role, 67

Xerox, 85

Yudof, M., 16, 18, 24

Zeiss, T., 53, 54, 89, 90
Zemsky, R., 17
Zook, G., 82

Back Issue/Subscription Order Form

Copy or detach and send to:

Jossey-Bass, A Wiley Imprint, 989 Market Street, San Francisco CA 94103-1741

Call or fax toll-free: Phone 888-378-2537 6:30AM – 3PM PST; Fax 888-481-2665

Back Issues: Please send me the following issues at $29 each
(Important: please include ISBN number with your order.)

_____

_____

_____

$ _____   Total for single issues

$ _____   SHIPPING CHARGES: SURFACE   Domestic Canadian
                           First Item $5.00 $6.00
                       Each Add'l Item $3.00 $1.50
For next-day and second-day delivery rates, call the number listed above.

Subscriptions   Please __ start __ renew my subscription to *New Directions for Community Colleges* for the year 2____at the following rate:

U.S.	__ Individual $80	__ Institutional $165
Canada	__ Individual $80	__ Institutional $165
All Others	__ Individual $104	__ Institutional $239
Online Subscription		__ Institutional $165

**For more information about online subscriptions visit
www.interscience.wiley.com**

$ _____   Total single issues and subscriptions (Add appropriate sales tax for your state for single issue orders. No sales tax for U.S. subscriptions. Canadian residents, add GST for subscriptions and single issues.)

__Payment enclosed (U.S. check or money order only)
__VISA __ MC __ AmEx __ # _____Exp. Date _____

Signature _____ Day Phone _____
__ Bill Me (U.S. institutional orders only. Purchase order required.)

Purchase order # _____
               Federal Tax ID13559302   **GST 89102 8052**

Name _____

Address _____

_____

Phone _____ E-mail _____

For more information about Jossey-Bass, visit our Web site at www.joss eybass.com

OTHER TITLES AVAILABLE IN THE
NEW DIRECTIONS FOR COMMUNITY COLLEGES SERIES
Arthur M. Cohen, Editor-in-Chief
Florence B. Brawer, Associate Editor

CC123 **Help Wanted: Preparing Community College Leaders in a New Century**
William E. Piland, David B. Wolf
This issue brings together various thoughtful perspectives on the nature of
leading community colleges over the foreseeable future. Authors offer
suggestions for specific programmatic actions that community colleges
themselves can take to provide the quantity, quality, specializations, and
diversity of leaders that are needed.
ISBN: 0-7879-7248-7

CC122 **Classification Systems for Two-Year Colleges**
Alexander C. McCormick, Rebecca D. Cox
This critically important volume advances the conversation among
researchers and practitioners about possible approaches to classifying two-
year colleges. After an introduction to the history, purpose, practice, and
pitfalls of classifying colleges and universities, five different classification
schemes are presented, followed by commentary by knowledgable
respondents representing potential users of a classification system:
community college associations, institutional leaders, and researchers. The
final chapter applies the five proposed schemes to a sample of colleges for
purposes of illustration.
ISBN: 0-7879-7171-5

CC121 **The Role of the Community College in Teacher Education**
Barbara K. Townsend, Jan M. Ignash
Illustrates the extent to which community colleges have become major
players in teacher education, not only in the traditional way of providing the
first two years of an undergraduate degree in teacher education but in more
controversial ways such as offering associate and baccalaureate degrees in
teacher education and providing alternative certification programs.
ISBN: 0-7879-6868-4

CC120 **Enhancing Community Colleges Through Professional Development**
Gordon E. Watts
Offers a much needed perspective on the expanding role of professional
development in community colleges. Chapter authors provide descriptions
of how their institutions have addressed issues through professional
development, created institutional change, developed new delivery systems
for professional development, reached beyond development just for faculty,
and found new uses for traditional development activities.
ISBN: 0-7879-6330-5

CC119 **Developing Successful Partnerships with Business and the Community**
Mary S. Spangler
Demonstrates that there are many different approaches to community
colleges' partnering with the private sector and that when partners are
actively engaged in tailoring education, training, and learning to their
students, everyone is the beneficiary.
ISBN: 0-7879-6321-9

CC118   **Community College Faculty: Characteristics, Practices, and Challenges**
Charles Outcalt
Offers multiple perspectives on the ways community college faculty fulfill
their complex professional roles. With data from national surveys, this
volume provides an overview of community college faculty, looks at their
primary teaching responsibility, and examines particular groups of
instructors, including part-timers, women, and people of color.
ISBN: 0-7879-6328-3

CC117   **Next Steps for the Community College**
Trudy H. Bers, Harriott D. Calhoun
Provides an overview of relevant literature and practice covering major
community college topics: transfer rates, vocational education, remedial
and developmental education, English as a second language education,
assessment of student learning, student services, faculty and staff, and
governance and policy. Includes a chapter discussing the categories,
types, and purposes of literature about community colleges and the
major publications germane to community college practitioners and
scholars.
ISBN: 0-7879-6289-9

CC116   **The Community College Role in Welfare to Work**
C. David Lisman
Provides examples of effective programs including a job placement program
meeting the needs of rural welfare recipients, short-term and advanced levels
of technical training, a call center program for customer service job training,
beneficial postsecondary training, collaborative programs for long-term
family economic self-sufficiency, and a family-based approach recognizing
the needs of welfare recipients and their families.
ISBN: 0-7879-5781-X

CC115   **The New Vocationalism in Community Colleges**
Debra D. Bragg
Analyzes the role of community college leaders in developing programs,
successful partnerships and collaboration with communities, work-based
learning, changes in perception of terminal education and transfer
education, changing instructional practices for changing student populations
and the integration of vocational education into the broader agenda of
American higher education.
ISBN: 0-7879-5780-1

CC114   **Transfer Students: Trends and Issues**
Frankie Santos Laanan
Evaluates recent research and policy discussions surrounding transfer
students, and summarizes three broad themes in transfer policy: research,
student and academic issues, and institutional factors. Argues that
institutions are in a strategic position to provide students with programs for
rigorous academic training as well as opportunities to participate in formal
articulation agreements with senior institutions.
ISBN: 0-7879-5779-8

United States Postal Service

Statement of Ownership, Management, and Circulation

1. Publication Title	2. Publication Number	3. Filing Date
New Directions For Community Colleges	0 1 9 4 - 3 0 8 1	9/30/03

4. Issue Frequency	5. Number of Issues Published Annually	6. Annual Subscription Price
Quarterly	4	$80 Individual $165 Institution

7. Complete Mailing Address of Known Office of Publication (Not printer) (Street, city, county, state, and ZIP+4)

989 Market Street
San Francisco, CA 94103-1741
San Francisco County

Contact Person
Joe Schuman
Telephone
415 782 3232

8. Complete Mailing Address of Headquarters or General Business Office of Publisher (Not printer)

Same as above

9. Full Names and Complete Mailing Addresses of Publisher, Editor, and Managing Editor (Do not leave blank)

Publisher (Name and complete mailing address)

Wiley, San Francisco
Jossey-Bass - Pfeiffer
Address - same as above

Editor (Name and complete mailing address)

Arthur M. Cohen
Eric Clearinghouse for Community Colleges
3051 Moore Hall Box 95121
Los Angeles, CA 90095-1521

Managing Editor (Name and complete mailing address)

None

10. Owner (Do not leave blank. If the publication is owned by a corporation, give the name and address of the corporation immediately followed by the names and addresses of all stockholders owning or holding 1 percent or more of the total amount of stock. If not owned by a corporation, give the names and addresses of the individual owners. If owned by a partnership or other unincorporated firm, give its name and address as well as those of each individual owner. If the publication is published by a nonprofit organization, give its name and address.)

Full Name	Complete Mailing Address
John Wiley & Sons Inc.	111 River Street Hoboken, NJ 07030

11. Known Bondholders, Mortgagees, and Other Security Holders Owning or Holding 1 Percent or More of Total Amount of Bonds, Mortgages, or Other Securities. If none, check box. ▶ ☑ None

Full Name	Complete Mailing Address
Same as above	Same as above

12. Tax Status (For completion by nonprofit organizations authorized to mail at nonprofit rates) (Check one)
The purpose, function, and nonprofit status of this organization and the exempt status for federal income tax purposes:
☐ Has Not Changed During Preceding 12 Months
☐ Has Changed During Preceding 12 Months (Publisher must submit explanation of change with this statement)

PS Form 3526, October 1999 (See Instructions on Reverse)

13. Publication Title	14. Issue Date for Circulation Data Below
New Directions For Community Colleges	Summer 2003

15.	Extent and Nature of Circulation	Average No. Copies Each Issue During Preceding 12 Months	No. Copies of Single Issue Published Nearest to Filing Date
a.	Total Number of Copies (Net press run)	1,307	1,248
b. Paid and/or Requested Circulation	(1) Paid/Requested Outside-County Mail Subscriptions Stated on Form 3541 (Include advertiser's proof and exchange copies)	781	734
	(2) Paid In-County Subscriptions Stated on Form 3541 (Include advertiser's proof and exchange copies)	0	0
	(3) Sales Through Dealers and Carriers, Street Vendors, Counter Sales, and Other Non-USPS Paid Distribution	0	0
	(4) Other Classes Mailed Through the USPS	0	0
c.	Total Paid and/or Requested Circulation (Sum of 15b. (1), (2),(3),and (4)] ▶	781	734
d. Free Distribution by Mail (Samples, compliment ary, and other free)	(1) Outside-County as Stated on Form 3541	0	0
	(2) In-County as Stated on Form 3541	0	0
	(3) Other Classes Mailed Through the USPS	1	1
e.	Free Distribution Outside the Mail (Carriers or other means)	162	161
f.	Total Free Distribution (Sum of 15d. and 15e.) ▶	163	162
g.	Total Distribution (Sum of 15c. and 15f) ▶	944	896
h.	Copies not Distributed	363	352
i.	Total (Sum of 15g. and h.) ▶	1,307	1,248
j.	Percent Paid and/or Requested Circulation (15c. divided by 15g. times 100)	83%	82%

16. Publication of Statement of Ownership
☐ Publication required. Will be printed in the Winter 2003 issue of this publication.
☐ Publication not required.

17. Signature and Title of Editor, Publisher, Business Manager, or Owner

Susan E. Lewis
VP & Publisher - Periodicals

Date 9/30/03

I certify that all information furnished on this form is true and complete. I understand that anyone who furnishes false or misleading information on this form or who omits material or information requested on the form may be subject to criminal sanctions (including fines and imprisonment) and/or civil sanctions (including civil penalties).

Instructions to Publishers

1. Complete and file one copy of this form with your postmaster annually on or before October 1. Keep a copy of the completed form for your records.

2. In cases where the stockholder or security holder is a trustee, include in items 10 and 11 the name of the person or corporation for whom the trustee is acting. Also include the names and addresses of individuals who are stockholders who own or hold 1 percent or more of the total amount of bonds, mortgages, or other securities of the publishing corporation. In item 11, if none, check the box. Use blank sheets if more space is required.

3. Be sure to furnish all circulation information called for in item 15. Free circulation must be shown in items 15d, e, and f.

4. Item 15h., Copies not Distributed, must include (1) newsstand copies originally stated on Form 3541, and returned to the publisher, (2) estimated returns from news agents, and (3), copies for office use, leftovers, spoiled, and all other copies not distributed.

5. If the publication had Periodicals authorization as a general or requester publication, this Statement of Ownership, Management, and Circulation must be published; it must be printed in any issue in October or, if the publication is not published during October, the first issue printed after October.

6. In item 16, indicate the date of the issue in which this Statement of Ownership will be published.

7. Item 17 must be signed.

Failure to file or publish a statement of ownership may lead to suspension of Periodicals authorization.

PS Form 3526, October 1999 (Reverse)